LEO THORN

The Author's Voyage

Contents

II Character Development

V   Editing And Revision

VI   Publishing And Marketing

Preface

Welcome to "The Author's Voyage: From First Draft To Bestseller". This book is designed to guide aspiring writers through every stage of the writing and publishing process, from developing a concept to promoting a finished book.

As an author myself, I know firsthand how daunting it can be to embark on the journey of writing a book. That's why I've created this guide, to provide a road map for writers who are just starting out or who have hit a roadblock in their creative process.

In "The Author's Voyage," you will find detailed information and practical tips on all aspects of writing and publishing, including getting started, character development, plotting and story structure, writing style and techniques, editing and revision, and publishing and marketing. Whether you're a first-time writer or a seasoned pro, there's something in this book for you.

Throughout the book, I draw on my own experiences and the wisdom of successful authors, editors, and publishers to provide you with a comprehensive guide to the writing process. Each chapter includes topics to help you apply the concepts to your own writing, and there are plenty of examples to illustrate key points.

Writing a book can be a challenging and rewarding experience, and I hope that "The Author's Voyage" will help make your journey a little easier. So grab a pen, open your mind, and let's set sail on the adventure of a lifetime.

Best wishes,

Leo Thorn

I

Getting Started

1

Create a writing schedule and stick to it

If you're a writer struggling to find the best time to write, there's a solution! You can try writing at different times of the day to determine when you feel most energetic and focused. If you tend to feel more alert at night, that's fantastic! You can allocate some time before going to bed to write, but ensure that you still get enough sleep. Paying attention to your body's natural patterns and finding a writing schedule that works best for you is important.

The Importance of Scheduling Writing Sessions

Making a schedule for writing helps you establish a consistent routine and structure your day to ensure you have enough time to devote to your writing. This can increase your productivity and allow you to steadily work towards completing your writing projects.

Ideal Length of Writing Sessions

The best writing session length varies from person to person. Some writers work better in short bursts of 30-45 minutes, while others prefer longer sessions of 2-3 hours. Whatever your preference, make sure you set aside enough time to make significant progress on your writing project.

Sticking to Your Writing Schedule

It can be difficult to follow a writing schedule, especially if you have a lot going on or are working on multiple projects. To stay on track, try setting goals for each writing session, such as writing a certain number of words or finishing a specific part of your project. You can also set reminders or alarms to help you stay focused and avoid getting distracted.

Making Writing a Non-Negotiable Priority

If you want to prioritize writing, you must treat it as an important task on your to-do list. Set aside specific times in your schedule for writing and treat them as unbreakable appointments. Inform your loved ones that you won't be available during these sessions, and avoid scheduling other activities during this time. This way, you can focus on writing without interruptions.

Setting Deadlines as a Writer

Deadlines are essential for writers because they keep us focused and help us stay on track. Knowing when we need to finish a writing project helps us prioritize our work and avoid putting things off. Setting deadlines also gives our writing a clear structure and sense of purpose, which can help us stay motivated and driven.

Dealing with Procrastination Despite Deadlines

Many writers struggle with procrastination, but there are

ways to overcome it. One effective method is to divide your writing project into smaller tasks and set deadlines for each task. This approach can help you focus on one task at a time, rather than feeling overwhelmed by the whole project.

Another way to overcome procrastination while writing is to set achievable goals for each session. For instance, you can aim to write a certain number of words or complete a particular scene. Setting goals can provide a clear sense of direction and motivation. Also, minimizing potential distractions like social media or email notifications can help you remain focused and avoid procrastination.

Always keep in mind that establishing deadlines and using tactics to overcome procrastination can help you achieve greater success and productivity as a writer.

2

Develop a writing routine to help you get in the zone

Having a writing ritual prepares your mind for writing by sending a signal that it's time to focus and be creative. Not only that, but a writing ritual can also help you feel more at ease and calm, which can minimize stress and anxiety. So why not try establishing a writing ritual for yourself? It can be as simple as lighting a candle or taking a few deep breaths before you start writing. See how it feels and experiment until you find a writing ritual that works best for you.

Examples of Writing Routines to Boost Productivity

You can have various writing rituals like scheduling a specific time and place to write, making a cup of tea or coffee before starting, lighting a candle or incense, or doing a brief meditation or breathing exercise. Select a writing ritual that suits you and that you can integrate into your writing routine consistently.

Importance of Selecting a Specific Time and Place for Writing

Choosing a fixed time and location for writing develops a

consistent writing routine. This way, you won't have to worry about making daily decisions on when and where to write, which can decrease decision-making exhaustion and keep you motivated to accomplish your writing objectives.

The Power of Music for Writing

Music can assist in generating a particular mood or ambience for your writing. Additionally, it can help you block out distractions and remain focused. Some writers discover that instrumental music or white noise is more beneficial, while others prefer music with lyrics. Try different types of music to determine which one works best for you.

How Freewriting Can Help You Get into the Writing Mindset

Freewriting is a writing method where you write continuously for a specific period without caring about grammar or structure. It's beneficial in overcoming writer's block and reaching a flow state where ideas can come more naturally. Freewriting also works as an excellent warm-up exercise to help you get into writing mode.

Tips for Consistency in Your Writing Routine

If you want to improve your writing skills, be consistent. Make it a habit to write at a particular time and place every day, even if it's only for a short time. Keep yourself responsible by setting achievable objectives and monitoring your advancement. Having a writing companion or accountability group can also help you stay motivated and stay on track with your writing goals.

Staying Motivated to Write Regularly

It can be hard to maintain the motivation to write regularly, but there are ways to help you stay motivated. One way is to set clear writing goals, and another is to have people around you who encourage and support you. Celebrating your writing successes with small rewards can also help you stay motivated. Don't forget to remind yourself why you started writing and how it can help you achieve your personal and professional aspirations.

The Importance of Developing a Habit of Writing Regularly
Writing on a regular basis can help you improve your writing skills and build momentum. This can keep you motivated and help you make progress on your writing projects. Plus, the more you write, the easier it becomes to get in the zone and produce high-quality work.

How Long Does it Take to Form a Writing Habit?
Developing a new habit can take about three weeks, but it can vary based on individual circumstances. Stay patient and motivated, even if you miss a day or two of writing. Consistent effort will make writing regularly become a habit over time.

What to Do When Your Writing Routine Isn't Working
If you're struggling with your writing routine, it's essential to figure out what's causing the problem. You might need to change your routine to fit your schedule or find a new place to write that helps you concentrate better. Review your writing goals and ensure they're realistic and significant to you.

Reviewing and Adjusting Your Writing Routine: How Often is Necessary?

To keep your writing routine effective, Regularly review and adjust it based on your progress and changing circumstances. You can do this every few weeks or months to evaluate your progress and make necessary changes. This will help you stay focused on your writing goals and maintain a consistent writing routine.

3

Write a detailed outline to help guide your writing process

An outline improves your writing process. It helps you structure your ideas and thoughts, making your writing smoother and more effective.

Essential Components of an Outline

The components of your outline may vary based on the specific writing project you're tackling. However, it's typical to include a concise statement of your main idea, the key concepts or arguments that uphold your main idea, and any corroborating evidence or illustrations. You might also consider incorporating any additional subtopics or particulars that endorse your central ideas.

Important elements to include in a story outline

When creating an outline for your story, there are certain important aspects to include. These may include the main characters and their motivations, the setting and its significance, and the key plot points that move the story forward.

Additionally, it's essential to think about the underlying message or theme you want to communicate, which can help you maintain clarity and coherence in your storytelling.

Organizing Thoughts with an Outline

An outline is like a map that guides you while you write. It arranges your ideas in a way that makes sense and helps you see the overall picture of your story. By creating an outline, you can spot any problems with your plot, characters, or pace early on, and avoid wasting time and effort later on.

Benefits of Using an Outline in Writing

Using an outline has multiple advantages. It keeps you on track with the main idea of your story, assists you in developing your characters and plot in a seamless way, and prevents writer's block by providing a clear path to follow. Moreover, it can help you recognize any problems in your story beforehand, which can save you a lot of time and frustration.

Updating Your Outline as You Write

It's not uncommon for writers to stray from their original outline while writing, and that's perfectly fine. If you get a new idea or your story takes a different direction, you can update your outline to incorporate these changes. This can help you stay focused and avoid getting bogged down in the details.

Deviating from an outline or mind map while writing

It's alright to make changes to your outline or mind map if you think it's best for your story. But after making changes, you should remember to update your outline or mind map accordingly. This will help you keep track of your progress and make sure that you haven't missed anything important for your plot or characters.

Staying Focused on the Main Theme or Idea with an Outline

Make sure to include the main message or idea of your story in your outline. This can act as a helpful compass while you write, allowing you to keep your story on track and true to its core message.

A suggested structure or framework for creating an outline

There are different ways to outline a story, such as the three-act structure that includes an introduction, rising action, climax, falling action, and resolution. Another method is using a beat sheet, which breaks the story into individual beats or moments that help move the plot forward. The best outlining method depends on your writing style and the story's needs.

The timing of outlining in the writing process: before starting or as you go

Although some writers prefer to dive straight into writing without a plan, I suggest creating a simple outline beforehand to keep you on track and prevent writer's block. However, it's also important to remain adaptable and willing to make changes as you go along, as your story may take on a life of its own.

Mind-mapping tools for writing organization

A mind-mapping tool is a visual aid that assists in organizing ideas and thoughts. It permits you to link distinct ideas and concepts in a logical manner. You can begin with a core idea and branch out to different subtopics, plot points, characters, and more.

Using a mind map or detailed outline is helpful in generating new ideas for your writing. Breaking your story down into different sub-topics and plot points will help identify areas that require more detail or development. With the aid of a mind map or outline, you can also explore different options for plot twists or character developments.

Improving writing with a detailed chapter-by-chapter outline

A detailed chapter-by-chapter outline can be really helpful for getting your story organized and making sure everything flows smoothly. By planning out what happens in each chapter, you can keep your plot on track and catch any problems before they become big issues. This way, you can be sure that your story makes sense from beginning to end.

Benefits of a structured approach to writing

Using a structured approach when writing has many advantages. It can save time and prevent writer's block, keep you focused and prevent feeling overwhelmed by the task at hand. A structured approach also helps you stay on track and work towards completing your writing goals.

Using an outline as a guide without feeling restricted

Remember that your outline is a tool to guide you, not a set of strict rules to follow. It's essential to have a plan, but also be open to making adjustments as needed. Your outline should be adaptable enough to allow for new ideas or changes that may arise while you're writing. Think of your outline as a map that you can veer off from or try different routes as you see fit.

4

Use mind-mapping or brainstorming techniques to generate ideas

If you're experiencing a lack of inspiration, don't worry, it's common. To generate new ideas, try mind mapping or brainstorming. Start by jotting down a main topic or idea and then branch out with related ideas or subtopics using words, phrases, or images. This technique can help you visualize your ideas and their connections. Additionally, taking a break from writing and engaging in inspiring activities like reading, listening to music, or going for a walk can help clear your mind and spark new ideas. Give it a try and see what works best for you.

Using Mind-Mapping or Brainstorming to Generate Writing Ideas

Mind mapping or brainstorming is an effective technique to generate fresh ideas because it lets you explore diverse aspects and associations of your main topic. Writing down ideas and branching out can lead you to new connections and unique viewpoints that you might not have considered before. This creative exercise enables you to unleash your imagination and create new ideas for your writing.

The Importance of Not Censoring Yourself When Brainstorming for Writing

Don't criticize or filter your ideas during brainstorming since it can restrict your creativity and decrease the likelihood of coming up with new concepts. During this phase, the objective is to produce as many ideas as possible, even if they sound ridiculous or unrealistic. It's vital to allow yourself the freedom to consider various options and perspectives without being concerned about their quality or accuracy. You can always improve and refine your ideas later. The aim of brainstorming is to unleash your imagination and discover potential opportunities.

Brainstorming Techniques for Generating Writing Ideas

There are various methods to generate ideas. Before you begin, determine your target audience and the type of writing you wish to create. This will aid you in directing your brainstorming efforts and ensuring that your ideas are pertinent to your desired readers.

Sparking Creativity with Mind-Mapping

Mind mapping involves creating a visual diagram that connects different concepts and themes related to your writing project. Begin with a central idea or theme and expand into subtopics or related concepts. This can help you get a clear understanding of your ideas and inspire you to come up with more creative solutions.

Using Writing Prompts to Generate Ideas

Writing prompts are questions or scenarios that are meant to inspire you to write. They can be found online, in books, or you can create your own. Writing prompts can help you generate new ideas and overcome writer's block.

Writing Exercises to Get Your Creative Juices Flowing

To boost your creativity, you can try various writing exercises. For instance, you can try free writing, where you write non-stop for a specific period without worrying about grammar or punctuation. Another option is to write a character sketch where you describe a character in detail or to write a scene from a different character's perspective.

What to Do with Brainstorming Notes: Turning Ideas into Action

After completing the brainstorming process, it's recommended to go through the notes and select the most interesting and relevant ideas. These can be used as a starting point for your writing project. Keep in mind that the brainstorming stage is just the beginning, and you may need to revise and improve your ideas as you progress with your writing.

5

Take inspiration from the world around you by people-watching or visiting new places

There are plenty of sources to draw from to find inspiration for your writing. Consider your own life experiences, current events, the natural world, art, music, and books. Unusual sources of inspiration can also come from dreams, conversations with strangers, or letting your imagination run wild. Keep an open mind and observe the world around you, and you'll be surprised at how many ideas you can generate. Give it a try and see where your imagination takes you.

The Power of Observation: Using the World Around You for Writing Inspiration

Watching and observing people and the world around you can be valuable for your writing. It can help you create more realistic characters and settings in your stories. It can also give you a better understanding of human emotions and behavior, which can add depth and complexity to your characters.

Exploring New Experiences: Ways to Gain Fresh Perspectives as a Writer

As a writer, you can gain new experiences by exploring different locations, such as a new city, country, or even just a new area in your own town. This can expose you to unique cultures, foods, and environments that can spark inspiration for your writing. Attending events like art exhibits, book readings, or music concerts can also provide new perspectives and ideas. Lastly, reading different genres and styles of writing can broaden your knowledge and inspire fresh ideas for your own writing.

6

Find a writing space that inspires you

Consider having a specific area for writing to increase your writing productivity. This can help your mind associate that area with the act of writing, making it easier to focus when you start working. Give it a try and see if it works for you.

Factors to Consider When Creating a Writing Space

When creating a writing space, it's essential to pick a place that suits your needs and is comfortable. It could be in your house, at a library, or even at a coffee shop. Ensure the space has proper lighting, such as natural light or warm, gentle lighting, to help reduce eye strain and create a soothing environment.

Tips for Creating a Comfortable and Distraction-Free Writing Space

To create a distraction-free writing space, get rid of anything that could distract you from your writing. This involves turning off your phone, minimizing noise, and keeping your workspace tidy. You may also want to consider getting a comfortable chair and desk and using tools such as noise-cancelling headphones to help you focus better on your writing.

Sources of Inspiration for Writing

It's important to have inspiration around you while writing to keep your creativity going. You can surround yourself with things that inspire you, like motivational quotes, pictures that spark your imagination, or even scents that give you energy.

Aromatherapy: Enhancing Your Writing Environment

Aromatherapy is the art of using pleasant scents to enhance your physical and mental health. Some smells like peppermint or lavender can alleviate stress and boost concentration. Putting essential oils or candles in your writing area can make a relaxed and invigorating environment.

How Ambient Noise Can Boost Your Writing

Some writers may find complete silence preferable, while others benefit from ambient noise to help them focus. White noise or instrumental music can be used to block out distractions and create a peaceful atmosphere. However, it's essential to find the right noise level for you, as excessive noise can be just as distracting as no noise at all.

7

Set realistic goals for yourself to stay motivated

Setting realistic goals is key to staying motivated and making progress on your writing project. Breaking the project into smaller, achievable goals can make the task feel less over-whelming. For example, if you're writing a novel, consider setting a goal to write a specific number of pages or chapters each week. Give it a try and see how much progress you can make.

Strategies for breaking a writing project into smaller, achievable goals

A helpful strategy is to make a list of tasks or a checklist. For instance, if your ultimate goal is to finish a novel, you can create a list of tasks that need to be completed like "create the story's outline," "develop the characters," "write the first draft," and "revise the manuscript." Breaking down a bigger goal into smaller tasks can make it feel more achievable and less daunting.

How deadlines and self-imposed time limits can help complete each goal

Setting deadlines or time limits for each goal can help you stay motivated and make steady progress. Set realistic deadlines though, to avoid becoming discouraged if you can't meet them. The goal is to make progress and stay motivated, not to overwhelm yourself.

Celebrating accomplishments along the way

Taking time to celebrate your progress can be a great way to stay motivated and inspired. You can choose rewards that are personal to you, like your favorite food, a break to watch a movie, or buying something small that you've had your eye on. The point is to choose something that makes you feel good about what you've accomplished.

What to do if falling behind on writing goals

It's normal to sometimes not meet your writing goals. If this happens, don't be too hard on yourself and try not to feel disheartened. Instead, take a moment to figure out what went wrong and make any necessary changes to your goals or schedule. Maybe you need more time to complete a task or need to adjust your writing schedule to fit your other responsibilities. Keep pushing forward and staying committed to your main goal.

Staying motivated and inspired while working on a long writing project

Staying motivated and inspired is important when working on a long writing project. You can stay motivated by reminding yourself of why you started writing it and what you hope to achieve by completing it. You can also take breaks and engage in other creative activities to recharge your creative energy. Establishing a writing routine can make it easier to get into the writing mindset and stay motivated. Additionally, joining a writing community or finding a writing partner can provide valuable feedback and support.

Tracking Your Writing Progress: Writing Journals and Productivity Apps

A writing journal can be an effective way to track your progress while writing. You can record your daily word count, and the tasks you've completed and reflect on your progress. Additionally, you can use productivity tools like Trello or Evernote to stay organized and on track.

The Importance of Regularly Reviewing Your Progress Towards Writing Goals

To stay on track with your writing goals, review your progress regularly, like once a week or a month. This can help you stay accountable and make adjustments to your approach. If you're struggling to meet your goals, it may be necessary to re-evaluate and change your writing process. Set goals that challenge you but are still attainable.

8

Identify your target audience before you start writing

Identify your target audience beforehand. Knowing who your readers are will allow you to write in a way that connects with them and meets their expectations. By understanding your readers' demographics, interests, and preferences, you can write a book that is engaging, useful, and relevant to them. This can greatly increase your chances of success.

Factors to Consider When Determining Your Ideal Reader

When identifying your ideal reader, you should take into account factors such as their age, gender, education level, occupation, interests, and values. You should also consider the genre and niche of your book, as well as the tone, style, and language you want to use. By analyzing these factors, you can create a profile of your ideal reader and write a book that will be relevant and engaging to them.

How Tailoring Your Writing Style, Tone, and Language to Your Target Audience Improves Your Writing

Adapting your writing style, tone, and language to your target audience can enhance your writing in various ways. Firstly, it can help you connect with your readers on a personal level, which makes your writing more relatable, interesting, and pleasurable to read. Secondly, it can aid you in communicating your message more effectively by utilizing language and instances that your readers are acquainted with. Finally, it can help distinguish your writing from other books in the same category by creating a distinct voice and style that appeals particularly to your intended audience.

Examples of Writing Styles that Might Appeal to Different Target Audiences

The writing style that would attract different target audiences could depend on the genre, niche, and reader demographics. For instance, a Young Adult book may use a casual and conversational tone, whereas a self-help book might be more formal and authoritative. A romantic novel could use more emotional and descriptive language, while a thriller could use more suspenseful and action-packed sentences. When choosing your writing style and tone, it's essential to consider your genre and target audience.

How Conducting Research on Your Target Audience Improves Your Writing

Researching your target audience can enhance your writing by providing you with valuable insights into your readers' likes, dislikes, and interests. This understanding allows you to customize your writing to cater to their needs, making your book more interesting and valuable to them. Moreover, it helps you identify potential gaps or unexplored opportunities in the market, enabling you to create a unique writing style and content that appeals to your readers.

Research Methods to Better Understand Your Target Audience

There are different ways to learn more about your target audience, including surveys, interviews, and focus groups where you can ask questions and gather feedback from your readers. You can also check online reviews and discussions related to your topic or genre, and analyze data about your readers, such as their age, gender, location, and reading preferences. These methods can help you better understand your audience and create content that resonates with them.

How Knowing Your Target Audience Helps with Marketing and Promotion

Understanding your target audience can help you effectively market and promote your writing. For instance, if you know your readers often use social media, you can concentrate on promoting your book through platforms like Facebook, Twitter, or Instagram. Similarly, if you're aware that your readers prefer audiobooks, you can prioritize creating an audio version of your book.

Utilizing Knowledge of Your Target Audience for Marketing and Promotion

When you know your target audience, you can market and promote your book in a way that appeals to their interests and needs. This means you can create marketing messages that are more compelling, select the appropriate platforms to promote your book and create ads that are targeted towards your ideal reader. Additionally, knowing your target audience can help you connect with your readers and build a community around your writing.

9

Take breaks to avoid burnout

Take regular breaks to keep your writing productivity high and prevent burnout. There are various activities that can help you unwind and re-energize during a writing project. For example, you could take a walk, do some gentle exercise, or practice mindfulness techniques. These activities can help you refresh your mind and boost your motivation to continue writing.

The Importance of Taking Breaks in Writing Projects and the Effects of Mental Fatigue on Productivity

Take breaks when working on a writing project because mental fatigue can harm your writing productivity. When you're feeling exhausted or stressed, it can be hard to concentrate and produce good quality work. By taking breaks, you can give your mind and body a chance to recover and recharge. This can help you feel refreshed and reinvigorated, allowing you to tackle your writing with renewed enthusiasm and creativity.

Tips for Taking Breaks During a Writing Session

There are a few things you can do to make the most of your

writing breaks. You could set a timer for a specific amount of time, find a calm and serene environment to unwind, and engage in activities that don't require a lot of brainpower. For instance, you could listen to soothing music, do some gentle stretching or yoga, or simply sit back and focus on your breathing. These activities can help you relax and recharge quickly, so you're ready to dive back into your writing with renewed energy.

How Taking Breaks Can Increase Overall Productivity in Writing Projects

Contrary to what you might think, taking breaks can actually boost your productivity when working on a writing project. By taking regular breaks, you can avoid feeling exhausted and stay focused and energetic throughout the day. This can help you create better quality work in a shorter amount of time and reduce the need for long breaks or time off due to burnout.

In summary, to maintain your writing productivity and avoid burnout, take breaks. Discover relaxing activities that help you recharge, take breaks frequently during writing sessions, and prioritize your mental and physical well-being. This approach can assist you in producing quality work while maintaining your creative energy throughout your writing project.

10

Set aside dedicated time for research to ensure accuracy in your writing

Research can be daunting to start. A helpful tip is to begin by figuring out what information you need to answer your research questions. This can help you stay on track and avoid getting sidetracked by irrelevant information.

Importance of Using Reputable Sources in Research

Use trustworthy sources like academic journals, books, and interviews with experts in your research. These sources are reliable and have been reviewed by professionals in the field. Properly citing these sources can also prevent plagiarism and show your understanding of the topic.

Organizing Research Materials and Sources

Stay organized and keep track of your sources when conducting research. You can use tools like Zotero or EndNote to store and organize your sources and to automatically generate citations and bibliographies. Alternatively, you can create a document or spreadsheet to record your sources and related information.

Common Mistakes to Avoid in Conducting Research for Writing Projects

When conducting research for writing projects, avoid relying on biased or inaccurate sources. Using such sources can lead to errors in your work and damage your credibility as a writer. Additionally, cite your sources properly to avoid plagiarism and maintain the integrity of your work. Always follow the citation guidelines for your project and double-check your citations to ensure accuracy.

Incorporating Research into Writing Routine for More Informed and Credible Content

Integrating research into your writing routine can enhance the quality and credibility of your work. By conducting extensive research and citing trustworthy sources, you can showcase your knowledge and expertise on the subject. Furthermore, research can help you identify any knowledge gaps and lead to more well-rounded and comprehensive writing.

11

Avoid distractions during your writing time by turning off notifications and finding a quiet place to work

As a writer, I have noticed that distractions can be either from outside or inside. External distractions can include notifications, phone calls, or people talking, while internal distractions may come from negative self-talk or feeling unmotivated. Pinpoint what's causing the distractions and find ways to minimize them during writing time.

Personal Preferences: Working in Quiet or Noisy Environments

Personally, when I'm writing, I like to have a quiet atmosphere. But, some writers find instrumental music or white noise helpful while writing. Ultimately, it depends on the writer's personal preferences.

Effective Tools and Techniques for Staying Focused While Writing

I've discovered some strategies that aid me in maintaining focus while writing. To begin, I turn off all of my notifications on both my phone and computer to avoid getting sidetracked. Additionally, I utilize a website blocker to prevent myself from accessing distracting websites. Moreover, I discovered that setting a specific objective for my writing session, such as reaching a certain word count or finishing a specific scene, helps me stay motivated and focused.

Balancing Focus and Self-Care During Long Writing Sessions

Taking breaks and self-care maintain their focus and productivity. Short breaks like stretching or walking can help avoid burnout and improve concentration. Drinking enough water, getting enough sleep, and taking necessary breaks are essential for a writer's well-being. By prioritizing self-care, writers can maintain their motivation and focus, leading to better writing outcomes.

12

Don't worry about writing the perfect first sentence. Just start writing and revise later.

Starting a piece of writing with a good first sentence sets the tone and captures the reader's interest. However, it's not necessary for the first sentence to be perfect. Begin writing and get your thoughts on paper.

The Power of a Good First Sentence

A great first sentence can establish the mood and capture the reader's interest, leading them to continue reading. It may create a sense of fascination or mystery. Nonetheless, not every piece of writing requires an extraordinary or attention-grabbing first sentence. Align the tone of the opening sentence with the tone of the entire work.

What is one common mistake people make when starting to write?

When beginning to write, many people make the mistake of

obsessing over crafting the perfect opening sentence. However, this can impede your creativity and slow down your progress. It's better to simply start writing and focus on editing and revising later.

What is the purpose of revision in the writing process?

When you revise your written work, you are making improvements to enhance the overall quality of your piece. It allows you to perfect your ideas, make your message clearer, and refine your language, resulting in a more organized and interesting final product.

How does it help to overcome writer's block?

It encourages you to start writing without worrying about writing a perfect piece. This can be helpful in overcoming writer's block as it takes the pressure off and allows you to freely write your thoughts and ideas without hindrance. This helps in getting your ideas to flow and building momentum.

How important is it to have a perfect first draft?

It's not necessary to have a flawless initial version of your writing. Instead, it can be more beneficial to focus on jotting down your ideas first and then work on improving and modifying them afterwards. This can prevent you from getting stuck on trying to make everything perfect and enable you to advance with your writing.

How to improve the overall quality of a written piece?

It aims to boost the quality of your written work by encouraging you to focus on generating ideas and writing them down. Later on, you can revise your work to make sure your message is clear, your language is refined, and your ideas are well-supported. Don't worry about perfection from the start. Just begin writing and revise later to enhance your work's overall quality.

13

Don't worry about getting everything right in the first draft – focus on getting the words down and revising later

It's common to feel overwhelmed or anxious when starting a writing project, but remember that the first draft is just the starting point. Rather than striving for perfection, concentrate on writing down your ideas and telling your story. You can always improve and polish your work later through revision and editing.

I always find myself editing as I go along. Is that a bad thing?

Stopping to edit while writing can negatively impact the writing process. It can interrupt the flow of your thoughts and may lead to writer's block. It's better to avoid editing and instead concentrate on writing your ideas down. You can always return to edit and refine your work later on.

Once I've finished my first draft, what are some tips for effectively editing it?

If you need to edit your work, the first step is to take a break and come back to it later with a fresh perspective. Another helpful tip is to read your work aloud, which can help you identify any awkward phrasing or pacing issues. Have a clear goal in mind for your edits, such as fixing plot holes or improving character development.

How can embracing the editing process help me improve as a writer overall?

Editing your work is an important part of improving your writing skills and producing higher-quality work. By carefully reviewing and making changes to your writing, you can gain valuable insight into what works and what doesn't, which can help you become a better writer and create more captivating stories.

How can allowing yourself to write badly and make mistakes help with writer's block?

One way to overcome writer's block is to give yourself permission to write poorly and make mistakes. By doing so, you can alleviate the pressure of perfectionism and focus on getting your ideas out more quickly, leading to a more productive and creative flow.

What are some strategies for overcoming the pressure to write a perfect first draft?

There are a few strategies you can use to overcome the pressure of writing a perfect first draft. For example, you can aim to write a specific number of words every day without worrying if they're good or bad. Another strategy is to use prompts or writing exercises to help get your creative juices flowing. Remember that you can always revise your work later.

How can embracing imperfection and the writing process overall help improve the quality of the final product?

When you accept that imperfection is a natural part of the writing process and concentrate on the journey of writing rather than just the outcome, you allow yourself to be more adventurous and innovative in your writing. This approach can lead to more imaginative and captivating writing, and ultimately a superior final product. Always keep in mind that writing is a process, and making mistakes along the way is perfectly acceptable.

14

Don't be afraid to ask for help or advice from other writers or writing groups.

If you're feeling isolated, know that you're not alone. Collaborating with other writers or joining a writing group can provide you with a sense of community and support. You'll be able to get constructive feedback on your work, learn new writing techniques, and find motivation and inspiration. Being part of a writing group can also help you connect with other writers, which can lead to exciting new opportunities. So don't hesitate to reach out and join a writing community – it could be just what you need to take your writing to the next level.

How Writing Workshops and Conferences Can Improve Your Craft

Writing workshops and conferences can provide valuable learning experiences for writers. Workshops offer specialized instruction on specific writing techniques or genres, while conferences provide a range of panels and speakers covering various writing-related topics. These events can help writers improve their skills, gain insight into the publishing industry, and network with other writers and professionals.

How Connecting with Other Writers Can Boost Motivation and Inspiration

Writing can feel lonely at times, but connecting with other writers can bring a sense of togetherness and motivation. Sharing experiences, ideas, and feedback with other writers can spark creativity and new approaches to writing. It's comforting to have a supportive community of fellow writers who understand the challenges of writing and can offer encouragement and guidance when needed.

Resources for Finding Writing Groups and Online Communities

There are many resources and websites that writers can use to find writing groups or communities. Examples include Meetup.com, where you can search for groups by genre or location, and Writer's Digest, which provides a variety of resources and forums for writers. Social media platforms like Facebook groups and subreddit threads are also great options for connecting with other writers online.

Networking and Building Relationships with Other Writers for Career Growth and Publishing Opportunities

Making connections with other writers can open up doors for collaborations, feedback, and publishing opportunities. It's also useful to connect with writers who are more experienced and can provide guidance and connections. Attending writing events or conferences can also help you meet industry professionals such as agents and editors, which can be valuable in the publishing process.

Benefits of Joining a Local Writing Group or Attending Writing Workshops

By joining a local writing group or attending writing workshops, you can receive helpful feedback and constructive criticism on your writing, while also connecting with other writers and industry professionals. Attending these workshops can also help you enhance your writing skills by practicing and learning new techniques from experienced instructors.

How Online Writing Forums Can Help Writers: A Look at Reddit and Facebook Writing Groups

For writers who cannot join local writing groups or attend workshops, online writing groups can be a helpful alternative. These groups enable writers to share their work and receive feedback from a community of writers, in addition to fostering connections and discussions on various writing-related topics. They can also provide information on industry news and opportunities.

Writing Coaches and Editors: Their Role in Improving Writing Skills

A writing coach or editor is someone who helps writers improve their writing skills and the quality of their work. They provide advice and feedback on different aspects of writing, such as idea generation, sentence structure, and organization. Working with a coach or editor can help writers identify areas of improvement and develop their writing skills to produce better work.

Incorporating Feedback and Guidance into Your Writing Routine for Improved Writing Skills and Success

Regularly incorporating feedback and guidance from other writers or professionals can help writers develop their skills and improve the quality of their writing. By receiving critiques and feedback, writers can identify areas where they need to improve and learn from the experiences of others. Connecting with other writers can also provide opportunities for collaboration and growth and access to industry news and opportunities. In short, seeking out feedback and guidance is an essential component of successful writing practice.

15

Use prompts or writing exercises to jump-start your creativity when you're feeling stuck.

A writing prompt can be a helpful tool for inspiration to start writing. It provides a topic, idea, or image to jump-start your creativity and get you writing. Give it a try and see where your imagination takes you!

Can Writing Prompts Help with Writer's Block and Generating New Ideas?

Writing prompts can be a fantastic way to break through writer's block and stimulate your imagination. Writing prompts provide you with a starting point or concept that you can expand on to create a story or written piece. Using prompts can encourage you to think creatively and push your boundaries.

How Setting a Timer Can Help with Writing Productivity

Using a timer helps to keep you focused and avoid distractions. When you set a time limit for your writing, it creates a sense of urgency that can help you make the most of your writing time. Also, it helps to break down a larger writing project into smaller, more manageable pieces. For instance, you can set a timer for 20 minutes and challenge yourself to write as much as you can during that period. Once the timer goes off, you can take a short break and then repeat the process. This can boost your writing ability and increase your confidence in writing efficiently and proficiently.

What are some Resources or Websites where Writers can find Writing Prompts?

There are numerous resources for writers seeking writing prompts, such as websites, books, and apps. Websites like Writer's Digest, Poets & Writers, and Creative Writing Now offer writing prompts. Writing accounts or hashtags on social media platforms like Twitter and Instagram also provide prompts.

How can Incorporating Writing Prompts into a Regular Writing Routine Help Improve Overall Writing Skills and Productivity?

Regularly using writing prompts can improve your overall writing skills and productivity in multiple ways. By practicing with prompts, you can enhance your creativity, improve your writing technique, and build your writing endurance. Writing prompts can also help you broaden your writing horizons by encouraging you to experiment with new styles and perspectives. Furthermore, using prompts regularly can help you establish a consistent writing routine, which is important for maintaining your writing momentum and productivity.

Choosing the Right Type of Prompts for Your Writing

To maximize the benefits of writing prompts, it's advisable to search for prompts that align with your writing interests or goals. For instance, if you intend to write horror stories, you should look for horror writing prompts. This will help you stay on track and improve your skills in your preferred genre or style.

Creating Your Own Writing Prompts

Make your own writing prompts to tailor your writing practice to your personal preferences and target areas where you want to grow. You can generate prompts by drawing inspiration from a variety of sources, such as themes, characters, settings, or anything else that sparks your creativity.

16

Experiment with different writing tools and mediums to find what works best for you

There are many different writing tools and technologies available for writers to try out. Some of these include Microsoft Word, Scrivener, Google Docs, and even traditional pen and paper. Every writer is unique and may prefer different tools based on their personal writing process and preferences.

Benefits of Writing Longhand or Using a Typewriter

Writing longhand with a pen and paper or using a typewriter can offer some benefits for writers. For instance, some writers feel more connected with their ideas and are able to concentrate better when using these tools. Typewriters and writing by hand also have a certain charm that some writers find appealing and inspirational.

How Writing Software Can Help Writers: Scrivener and Google Docs

Writing software like Scrivener and Google Docs can help writers be more organized and productive. Scrivener has features that allow writers to easily manage their writing projects, including organization tools and note-taking capabilities. Google Docs allows for seamless collaboration with others and automatic saving to the cloud. These tools also offer useful features like word count and formatting options.

Factors to Consider When Choosing a Writing Tool or Technology

When choosing a writing tool, personal preference is crucial, but you should also think about the type of writing project you have. Some tools are ideal for specific types of writing, like Scrivener for lengthy projects such as novels, while Google Docs are suitable for shorter projects or teamwork. Additionally, you should factor in the features you need, like simplicity, formatting, or offline accessibility.

How Experimenting with Writing Tools Can Improve Writing Skills

Trying out different writing tools and technologies can be beneficial for writers to discover what works best for them. It can also help them find new features and techniques that can improve their writing skills and productivity. By experimenting with various tools, writers may be able to write more efficiently and creatively, ultimately enhancing their overall writing experience.

17

Write in short bursts if you don't have large blocks of time available.

Many writers face difficulty finding large chunks of time to write due to their busy schedules. However, writing in short intervals whenever you can spare a few minutes can be a helpful technique. Even writing for just 10-15 minutes at a time can make a difference in the long run.

Ideal Length for Writing Sessions with a Timer

The duration of your writing sessions depends on your schedule and what you find comfortable. You can opt for shorter writing sessions of around 10-20 minutes or longer ones of 30-60 minutes. Try out different options to discover what suits you the best.

Determining the Daily Writing Time Needed

The time you spend writing each day depends on your schedule and goals. Some writers dedicate a few minutes every day, while others set aside an hour or two. The key is to establish achievable goals and maintain consistency in your writing routine.

How Breaks Can Boost Productivity and Focus

Taking breaks during writing sessions is actually helpful for staying productive and focused. Giving your brain a break allows it to rest and perform better. Breaks can also prevent burnout and improve your overall writing experience by providing time to recharge and think of new ideas.

Strategies for Maximizing Writing Sessions with a Timer

In order to maximize your writing sessions when using a timer, remove any potential distractions and concentrate entirely on your writing. This involves turning off your phone and other electronic devices, closing unnecessary tabs and applications, and setting up a peaceful workspace. Furthermore, you can establish specific objectives or prompts for each session, such as composing a specific amount of words or focusing on a particular plot point or character.

Benefits of Incorporating Timed Writing Sessions into a Regular Writing Routine

Including timed writing sessions into your writing routine on a regular basis can have a positive impact on your productivity and writing skills. Consistently engaging in short bursts of writing, even if only for a few minutes, helps to develop a habit and increase focus. Additionally, using a timer aids in time management and helps to establish a steady writing practice, which can boost writing skills.

Tools and Apps for Meeting Daily Writing Goals

You can use various tools and apps to help you stay on track with your daily writing goals. Some popular options are Write or Die, which uses negative feedback to encourage consistent writing, and Forest, which helps you stay focused by growing a virtual tree while you write. Additionally, setting a timer during each writing session can also help you stay focused and avoid distractions.

Motivating Yourself to Write Consistently

To keep yourself motivated to write consistently, it can be useful to set clear goals that are measurable, like writing a certain number of words each day. You can also establish a routine and write at the same time or in the same place every day to make it a habit. Remember to acknowledge and reward yourself for achieving your goals, whether it's with something small or simply taking pride in your progress.

18

Consider dictating your story using voice-to-text software if you prefer speaking to writing.

Using voice-to-text software can be very helpful for writers who prefer talking instead of typing. Some well-known voice-to-text options are Dragon NaturallySpeaking, Google Docs Voice Typing, and Apple Dictation. Just keep in mind that you may need to teach the software to understand your voice and accent properly.

How Using Voice-to-Text Software Can Benefit Your Writing Process?

Using voice-to-text software can make your work more efficient. It allows you to express your ideas faster and with less effort than typing or writing by hand. This is because speaking comes more naturally to most people, making it easier to capture your thoughts as they come to mind.

Moreover, using dictation through voice-to-text software can assist you in maintaining a seamless stream of thought and expression. This can be tricky when concentrating on spelling and grammar while writing. By eliminating these roadblocks, voice-to-text software enables you to convey your thoughts more completely and refine your writing further.

Tips for Practicing Clear and Concise Speech When Dictating with Voice-to-Text Software

There are some tricks that can help you enhance your dictation abilities. For instance, practicing speaking slowly and distinctly, and emphasizing each word clearly can be beneficial. Additionally, taking brief breaks between phrases or sentences can aid the software in keeping up with your speech. Another useful tip is to say punctuation marks out loud while dictating, such as "period" or "comma." This technique can help you avoid writing long, complex sentences that may be difficult to read.

Concerns About Errors in Voice-to-Text Software

Voice-to-text software isn't always flawless. Occasionally, it can make mistakes or misunderstand what you say. Nevertheless, many programs are built to learn and progress with usage, meaning that the more you use them, the more accurate they become in transcribing your speech. To reduce errors, it's best to use the software in a peaceful setting, devoid of noise or disruptions. Additionally, you can check your text thoroughly after dictating to detect any errors that might have gone unnoticed.

How Incorporating Voice-to-Text Software into a Writing Routine Can Boost Productivity and Writing Skills

Voice-to-text software makes writing simpler and more

accessible, allowing you to establish a more productive routine. You may discover that dictating helps you write faster and with less difficulty, ultimately enabling you to produce more work in less time. Moreover, dictation frees your mind from focusing on the technicalities of writing, allowing you to concentrate on generating innovative and compelling content. Overall, voice-to-text software is an excellent choice for writers who want to increase their productivity and streamline their writing process. Although it may require some practice, many writers find that it's an effort well spent.

Incorporating Physical Activity into Your Writing Routine While Dictating

If you prefer dictating your story using voice-to-text software, you can incorporate physical activity into your writing routine by walking, stretching or pacing around your room while dictating. Ensure that your device can pick up your voice clearly and that you're in a quiet environment.

19

Take care of yourself by getting enough sleep, exercise, and healthy food to fuel your creativity

Some self-care activities that can be helpful for writers include getting enough sleep, engaging in regular physical activity, and eating healthy, nutritious foods to fuel their creativity. Furthermore, practicing mindfulness or meditation can help reduce stress and enhance your ability to concentrate.

Importance of Self-Care for Writers

Writing can be exhausting, both mentally and emotionally. It's natural to feel pressured to produce, but ignoring self-care can result in burnout, which negatively impacts your mental, emotional, and physical health. Taking care of yourself helps you sustain your creativity, avoid burnout, and maintain a healthy balance between your writing goals and your personal well-being.

Tips for Balancing Self-Care and Writing

Taking care of yourself is just as important as writing. You can schedule self-care activities like taking breaks throughout the day to stretch or go for a walk, or you can set aside a specific time in your schedule for self-care. Listen to your body and take a break if you're feeling tired or overwhelmed. Remember, self-care is a must, not a luxury!

Signs of Burnout for Writers to Watch Out For

When you experience burnout, you may feel tired, unmotivated, and uninspired. It can also cause emotional exhaustion, and sometimes, physical symptoms like headaches or stomachaches. It's essential to be aware of these warning signs and take necessary steps to avoid burnout, as it can have negative impacts on your health and well-being.

Benefits of Incorporating Self-Care into Your Writing Routine

By taking care of yourself, you're not only boosting your physical, emotional, and mental health, but also your creativity and productivity as a writer. With self-care, you can decrease stress and increase focus, which ultimately leads to better work quality in a shorter time frame. Moreover, integrating self-care into your routine allows for a harmonious balance between your writing and personal life, leading to sustainable success in the long run.

20

Free-write to get your creative juices flowing

Freewriting is a way of writing where you just let your thoughts flow out onto the page without worrying about making mistakes or fixing them. The idea is to keep writing non-stop for a certain amount of time, so you can come up with lots of ideas and words. You don't need to stop or edit as you go along. Just keep writing whatever comes to mind.

How Setting a Timer Can Improve Your Writing Productivity

When you set a timer for a certain amount of time, it can boost your productivity when writing. This is because having a deadline helps you concentrate and get rid of any distractions. You commit to writing for a particular time, which allows you to stay focused on your writing and produce more.

Examples of Writing Prompts for Freewriting Exercises

There are many topics you can use to start freewriting. For instance, you can write about a memory that stands out to you, a character you created in your mind, or anything that you find fascinating. The key is to write without any restrictions or boundaries, allowing your thoughts to flow freely.

The Importance of Writing Continuously During Freewriting

Writing without stopping during freewriting helps to unlock your creativity and clear your mind. When you write without holding back, you allow yourself to come up with fresh ideas and thoughts that you may have never considered before. It's like giving your brain the freedom to explore new territories.

How Freewriting Can Overcome Writer's Block and Creative Challenges

If you're struggling with writer's block or creative challenges, freewriting can help you get unstuck. It works as a tool to jump-start your writing by allowing you to write freely without any pressure or criticism. This can help break down mental barriers and spark new ideas that can inspire you to write with more ease.

What to Do with Freewriting Notes After a Session

After finishing a freewriting session, you can go through your notes and pick out any ideas or phrases that catch your attention. These notes can be used as a foundation for your writing, or they can serve as inspiration for future projects. It's like mining for gold - you sift through the notes to find the most valuable nuggets to use in your writing.

Using Freewriting as a Warm-Up Exercise to Get into the Writing Mindset

Using freewriting as a warm-up exercise is a great way to get in the mood for writing. It helps to get your creative juices flowing by allowing you to write without any pressure or rules. This can help prepare you for more focused writing later on. Overall, freewriting is an excellent tool that can help writers at any level. It can boost your productivity, help you overcome creative blocks, and generate fresh ideas. Why not give it a shot and discover how it can benefit your writing practice?

Using Freewriting for Different Types of Writing: Is It Effective?

Freewriting is a versatile writing technique that can be applied to any type of writing, whether it's creative or academic. It can be helpful in generating ideas and overcoming writer's block, regardless of the specific type of writing you're working on.

Common Misconceptions About Freewriting: Debunking Myths and Misunderstandings

People sometimes think that freewriting is pointless because the writing is not perfect, but that's not true. The purpose of freewriting is to generate ideas and be creative, not to write perfectly. Another misconception is that freewriting doesn't work for everyone, but it can be helpful for any writer, regardless of their level of experience.

21

Read widely in your genre to get a sense of what works and what doesn't

Reading books in your chosen genre enhances your writing abilities. When you read widely, you can gain an understanding of what elements of a story are effective, such as the plot, character growth, and pace. You can also recognize the norms of the genre, which can be useful when you begin to write your own book.

Paying Attention to Key Elements When Reading in Your Genre

When reading books in your genre, focus on how the writer describes characters, settings, and conversations. Observe how they build up suspense, create well-rounded characters, and drive the story forward. It may also be helpful to make a note of the aspects you appreciate and those you don't so that you can refer to them in the future.

The Importance of Reading Widely Across Different Genres as a Writer

Reading a variety of genres can be beneficial for writers as it can help them to develop their unique writing style and voice. Exposure to different writing styles, story structures, and narrative techniques can inspire writers to think creatively and approach their writing in new ways.

Examples of Books or Authors That Have Influenced Writing

I've recently enjoyed "The Vanishing Half" by Brit Bennett, which expertly blends together various perspectives and timelines. I've also found Stephen King's books to be a helpful guide on how to create suspense and maintain a good pace. When it comes to developing characters and crafting clever conversations, I always turn to Jane Austen's novels for inspiration.

22

Surround yourself with supportive people who encourage your writing

Finding a supportive writing community can be difficult, but there are various options to explore. You can try looking for local writing groups or workshops, as well as online communities or forums, to connect with other writers. Attending writing conferences or taking classes can also help you meet other writers and industry professionals.

The Benefits of Sharing Your Work with Others

Sharing your writing with others can be very helpful. When you share your work with other writers or readers, you can get feedback that can help you improve your writing. You can also see how others react to your writing and get a better sense of how to improve it. It can also help you build confidence in your writing and motivate you to keep writing.

Giving and Receiving Constructive Feedback on Writing

Constructive feedback plays a significant role in writing. Offer feedback that focuses on the writing rather than the writer, and give specific feedback with both positive and negative points. While receiving feedback, one should listen attentively and try to understand it even if it's challenging. It's a good idea to ask questions and clear up any doubts.

The Benefits of Online Writing Groups or Classes

Joining online writing groups or classes can be a convenient way to get feedback on your writing and connect with other writers. It's especially useful for writers who don't have access to local writing communities. Online classes are often led by experienced writers or industry professionals who can offer valuable insights and guidance to help you improve your writing.

The Importance of Having a Supportive Writing Community

As a writer, it's common to feel isolated and face difficulties in the writing process. Therefore, having a community that understands and supports your craft can be incredibly beneficial. Being part of a supportive community can offer encouragement, motivation, and constructive feedback to help you improve your writing skills. It also provides opportunities for networking, learning, and personal growth as a writer. With a community, you'll feel more connected and less alone in your writing journey, which can help you stay committed to achieving your writing goals.

II

Character Development

23

Create relatable and dynamic characters

Creating characters that readers can relate to gives your characters flaws, which makes them more human and relatable. It's also important for your characters to have clear motivations, like wanting love, power, or freedom. Their actions and decisions should also make sense within the story.

How to Make Your Characters Dynamic

A dynamic character is one that goes through big changes and grows during the story. To make your characters dynamic, you can give them a flaw or weakness that they need to work on. You can also create challenges or problems for them to face that push them to change and develop. Remember that dynamic characters don't have to be heroes, they can be villains or supporting characters too.

The Importance of Relatable Characters

It's important for readers to feel a connection with the characters in a story. Characters that are relatable help readers feel empathy and an emotional connection with the story, which makes it more interesting and memorable. When readers can relate to a character, they become more interested in their journey and are more likely to care about what happens to them in the end.

Examples of Relatable Characters from Literature and Film
An excellent example of a relatable character is Katniss Everdeen from "The Hunger Games" books and movies. She's relatable because she has flaws like being impulsive, insecure, and anxious. Many readers can connect with her motivation to protect her loved ones. As she grows and changes throughout the series, she becomes a dynamic and fascinating character.

Techniques for Creating Multi-Dimensional Characters
To create multi-dimensional characters, there are a few things you can do. Firstly, you can give them an interesting backstory that explains their personality and motivations. You can also use conversations and interactions with other characters to show different sides of them. Adding quirks or unique traits to your characters makes them more relatable and realistic. Ensure their actions and decisions make sense for their personality and motivations, and that they grow and change as the story progresses.

24

Give your characters distinct personalities and voices

Create unique personalities for your characters to make them stand out and feel like real people by giving each character a backstory that shapes their behavior, beliefs, and motivations. This will help you create a well-rounded character with depth and complexity. You can also differentiate characters through their unique traits and quirks. For instance, a shy character may have nervous habits like biting their nails, while a confident character may stand tall and make bold gestures. These subtle differences make your characters more unique and memorable.

How to Differentiate Your Characters' Voices in Dialogue

Voice is crucial for creating distinctive characters. To differentiate their voices, you can use different speech patterns, slang, and vocabulary. Each character may have a unique way of speaking based on their background, education, and personality. For instance, a streetwise character may use a lot of slang, while a more educated character may speak more formally. Moreover, different characters may have different rhythms and patterns in their speech, such as speaking quickly or slowly, using long or short sentences, or repeating certain phrases or words.

How a Character's Personality Affects Their Word Choices and Mannerisms

A character's personality can affect how they speak and behave. A happy character may use positive language and have a cheerful tone, while a sad character may use negative words and speak quietly. The way a character moves and behaves can also show their personality. For example, a shy character may avoid eye contact or fidget, while a confident character may stand tall and look directly at others. By paying attention to these small details, you can make your characters seem more realistic and relatable.

Using Character Quirks and Idiosyncrasies to Make Them Memorable

Giving your characters quirky habits or behaviors can make them more memorable and interesting. You can think of small things that make each character unique, such as their favorite food or drink, the way they laugh, or a certain gesture they make when they're happy or anxious. These quirks add depth to your characters and help readers connect with them on a more personal level.

Examples of Characters with Distinct and Memorable Personalities.

There are many great characters in books that readers remember long after they finish the story. For example,

Holden Caulfield in "The Catcher in the Rye" is a unique and beloved character who stands out with his rebellious personality and sarcastic sense of humor. Hermione Granger from "Harry Potter" is another great example of a memorable character who is intelligent, loyal, and has a quick wit. Her love of books and correcting people's grammar make her even more endearing.

25

Develop your characters' backstories to add depth

Make your characters more complex and compelling by creating detailed backstories for them. By exploring a character's past experiences, relationships, and motivations, you can create a more realistic and relatable character. This can help readers connect with your characters on a deeper level and become more invested in their story.

Understanding the Importance of a Character's Backstory

A character's past can help readers understand their present actions and decisions. It also allows readers to connect with the character on an emotional level, as it provides insight into the character's previous challenges and experiences. This understanding can make the character's journey more meaningful and relatable.

How a Character's Backstory Can Add Depth to Your Story

Creating a detailed backstory for a character can make them more intricate and multi-dimensional, going beyond their surface-level characteristics and behaviors. Additionally, it can add to the story's tension and drama, particularly if the character's past has influenced their beliefs or values that clash with other characters or plot developments.

Elements to Include in a Character's Backstory

To create a well-rounded backstory for your character, you can think about various elements such as their family background, childhood experiences, education or training, past relationships, significant life events, and any traumatic incidents. These elements should be carefully chosen, based on their relevance to the story, and should help shape the character's personality and motivations.

When to Reveal a Character's Backstory in Your Story

It depends on the story's needs and the writer's preference. Introducing a character's backstory in the beginning can quickly capture readers' interest and create empathy, while revealing it slowly can build suspense and maintain readers' engagement. The timing of the reveal should feel organic and enhance the story.

Revealing Character Backstory: Balancing Information with Engagement

One way to reveal a character's backstory is by showing it naturally through their behavior and words. For instance, instead of directly telling readers that a character had a difficult childhood, you can reveal this information by portraying the character's fear and avoidance towards particular situations, and slowly uncover more about their past as the story unfolds.

How a Character's Backstory Can Change Throughout Your Story

Similar to real people, characters can change and develop based on what they experience. Although their backstory might be presented in a certain way at the beginning of the story, as they encounter new situations and relationships, their views might change or their recollections could be questioned. This can create intriguing plot twists and character growth.

Using Character Backstory to Create Conflict and Drive Plot

A character's past can create tension and interest in the plot. For instance, if a character has experienced disloyalty before, their trust issues may cause problems in their relationships with other characters. Similarly, if a character has undergone a traumatic experience in the past, their pursuit of redemption may lead to the story's plot.

Pitfalls to Avoid When Incorporating Backstory into Your Story

One mistake to avoid is giving too much backstory at once, which can be too much for readers to handle. Another mistake is adding a backstory that isn't relevant to the story or character development. Make sure the backstory you include has a purpose and helps to enrich the story.

Ensuring Character Backstory is Relevant and Valuable to the Story

To ensure a character's backstory is valuable, connect it to the story's main themes or conflicts. Consider how the character's past experiences shape their actions and motivations, and how it can contribute to the story's complexity and tension.

Using Backstory to Create Emotional Resonance with Readers

Sharing a character's backstory can be very impactful and emotional for readers. It helps them connect with the character on a deeper level by showing their past struggles, successes, and tragedies. This connection can help readers become more invested in the character's journey and evoke a stronger emotional response to the story. So, use backstory to create a powerful bond between readers and characters.

26

Think about how your characters' experiences shape their worldviews and actions

When you create a character for your story, think about where they come from and what they've been through. This can greatly affect how they see the world and the choices they make. By considering things like their family, culture, and past struggles, you can create characters that feel more real and interesting to readers. This can also make it easier for readers to understand and care about your characters.

How Experiences Shape a Character's Personality: An Example

Think about Harry Potter from the books by J.K. Rowling. He's had a tough life because he lost his parents and wasn't treated well by his new family. Plus, he found out he's a wizard! All of these things have made him the person he is today. Harry is really strong and likes to do things on his own. He cares a lot about his friends and always wants to do what's right.

Cultural and Socioeconomic Differences and Their Impact on Character Behavior

The way a character grew up and where they come from can really shape how they think and act. For example, someone from a culture where everyone works together might care more about the group's needs than their own. But someone from a culture where everyone is more focused on themselves might put their own needs first. Similarly, someone who grew up with fewer resources might be better at finding practical solutions to problems. But someone who grew up with a lot of privilege might be more confident and feel like they deserve more.

Utilizing Past Traumas to Influence Present Character Decisions

When bad things happen to a character in their past, it can really affect them in the present. For example, someone who was hurt by someone close to them might have a hard time trusting people and making good relationships. As a writer, you can use this information to make your characters more interesting and real. You can show how their past affects how they act and why they make the choices they do.

Adding Depth and Complexity through a Character's History

Taking the time to really understand a character's past and experiences can help you make them more interesting and complex. You can use this information to show why they act the way they do and what motivates them. By revealing bits of their backstory as the story goes on, you can keep readers interested and invested in the character. This can make for a more engaging and memorable story.

27

Show character growth and development throughout the narrative

Include character growth and development in your story. Otherwise, your characters may seem uninteresting or stagnant. The changes a character undergoes can occur over time or suddenly, but they must be realistic and fit with the character's personality.

Ways to Show a Character's Personal Growth and Change in a Story

There are many ways to show that a character is changing and growing throughout a story. Some of these include changes in the way they behave, their attitudes towards others, and the way they see the world around them. For instance, a character who starts off as self-centered and uncaring may begin to show more compassion and kindness towards others as the story progresses. You can also use symbols and images to represent the character's transformation, such as a caterpillar transforming into a beautiful butterfly.

Ensuring Believable and Consistent Character Growth in a Story

Introduce their personality traits and faults early in the story to make sure that your character's personal growth is believable. Throughout the story, their behavior and choices should be in line with these traits, even as they develop. Avoid sudden, unrealistic changes in the character's behavior or attitude. Instead, show a natural and gradual transformation that reflects the character's personality.

Using Character Growth to Make a Story More Impactful and Meaningful

When readers witness a character face and conquer challenges and develop into a better version of themselves, it can have a significant emotional impact on them. This can make the story more powerful and meaningful, and emphasize the story's underlying themes. However, ensure that the character's growth feels genuine and natural, rather than forced or artificial.

Using Actions and Decisions to Show Character Growth

To demonstrate a character's transformation, their decisions and actions throughout the story can be a powerful tool. Your character can encounter obstacles and make choices that reflect their growth and development. For instance, a character who is initially self-absorbed and narcissistic might learn to become more caring and empathetic as they progress through the story.

Examples of Key Decisions as Turning Points for Characters

A character's turning point alters their direction and leads to new possibilities. It might be a small decision, like confronting a bully, or a bigger one, like quitting their job or leaving home to explore new opportunities. These choices should be meaningful and have a noticeable effect on the character's growth.

Creating Moments of Crisis to Drive Character Growth

Create moments of crisis to encourage character development. These moments can involve a character facing something that goes against their beliefs, values or fears. It could be something that challenges them emotionally, physically, or mentally. These experiences should be significant enough to force the characters to re-evaluate their priorities and outlook on life.

Ensuring Character Growth is Consistent with Personality and Motivations

Ensure that a character's personal growth is in line with their existing traits and desires. For example, if your character is shy and introverted, their growth should reflect these qualities. You don't want your character to suddenly become outgoing and confident without a proper explanation. Make sure that the character's reasons for change are understandable and convincing.

Using Character Growth to Create a Satisfying Character Arc

A character arc that is satisfying shows the character's progress from the beginning of the story to the end. You can use the character's growth to create a fulfilling arc by showing how they have faced and conquered challenges, and how they have changed as a result. Make sure that the character's development is gradual and believable, and that it fits with the overall themes and messages of your story.

28

Avoid making your characters too perfect or heroic – flaws and weaknesses make them more relatable.

Characters that are imperfect and have weaknesses are more believable and relatable. No one is perfect, and readers can often connect with characters who face challenges and errors. Flaws can also create drama and tension in a story, as characters strive to overcome their weaknesses and face obstacles. Flaws and weaknesses, on the other hand, help to humanize characters and create an emotional connection between them and readers. Perfect characters can also make the story feel predictable and less engaging, as there is little room for conflict or unexpected plot twists.

How Flaws and Weaknesses Make Characters More Relatable

Readers can relate better to characters who have flaws and weaknesses because it shows that the character is like them, with imperfections and challenges. This can help readers to engage with the character and feel more invested in their story.

Additionally, flaws and weaknesses can provide a platform for a character to grow and evolve, which can be satisfying for readers to witness.

Flaws and Weaknesses as Strengths of Characters

A character's flaws and weaknesses can add depth and nuance to their personality, and they may even have strengths that are linked to their flaws. For instance, a character who is prone to anger may also possess strong leadership skills. It's essential to depict a character's complexities and how their flaws and weaknesses can impact their growth and development throughout the story.

Examples of Flawed Characters in Literature or Film

There are many characters in literature and film who have flaws and weaknesses. Some examples include Hamlet, who has a hard time making decisions and wants to get revenge, Holden Caulfield from "The Catcher in the Rye," who is negative and does things that harm himself, and Katniss Everdeen from "The Hunger Games," who has difficulty trusting others and forming emotional connections.

Balancing Flaws and Positive Traits to Create Well-Rounded Characters

If a character has too many flaws, it can be hard for readers to connect with them, but if they have no flaws, they may seem boring. By exploring a character's flaws and their impact on their actions, you can create an authentic and complex character.

To create a well-rounded character, balance their flaws with their positive traits. One way to do this is by demonstrating how a character's flaws can also be an advantage in certain circumstances. For instance, a character who is impulsive may make errors, but they may also be able to react quickly in an emergency. Additionally, showcasing a character's positive traits can make them more likeable and relatable, even with their flaws.

Creating Flaws in Characters Without Losing Likeability

To give characters flaws without making them unlikable, you can make their weaknesses understandable and relatable. For instance, a character who is too trusting can be taken advantage of by others, which is a relatable weakness that many people share. That way, readers can relate to them while still rooting for them.

Relatable Flaws to Add Depth to Characters

There are some common flaws that can make a character more likeable and relatable, such as arrogance, selfishness, jealousy, cowardice, impulsiveness, and dishonesty. These are all weaknesses that many people experience in their own lives, so readers can connect with characters who share these traits.

Complementary and Clashing Traits Among Characters

When a character's weaknesses and strengths work well with other characters in the story, it can create a sense of cooperation and teamwork. For instance, a character who acts impulsively can be balanced by another character who is more careful and strategic. However, when a character's flaws and strengths don't match well with others, it can create tension and conflict in the story. For example, two characters who are both stubborn may have different ideas about how to solve a problem, which can lead to a clash of opinions. Flaws can also create a power dynamic where one character has a flaw that another can use to their advantage.

Ensuring Distinct Personalities and Characteristics for Your Characters

Make sure that each of your characters has their own unique personality and traits, think about their backgrounds, experiences, and worldviews. Consider how their past has influenced their personality and outlook on life. You can also make each character more distinctive by giving them their own unique way of speaking, mannerisms, and quirks. Lastly, ensure that each character has their own goals and reasons for making certain choices throughout the story.

How Flaws Can Propel the Plot Forward: Examples

Flaws can move the story forward by making characters take wrong decisions that have a bad outcome. For instance, a character's arrogance may make them overlook a danger that leads to a disastrous consequence. On the other hand, a character's cowardice may make them freeze at a crucial moment, causing them to fail in their mission. Such situations can bring tension and drama to the story and keep the plot going.

Using Flaws to Illustrate Character Growth and Development

Flaws can be used to demonstrate a character's personal growth and development, which is very powerful, by having a character acknowledge their flaws and strive to improve themselves. For example, a selfish character may become more altruistic over the course of the story. Alternatively, a character may suffer a setback due to their flaws, but then learn from their mistakes and grow as a result. Portraying how a character can learn from their mistakes can add depth and richness to their character arc.

Examples of how flaws can make a character more interesting and complex

Flaws can make a character more interesting and complex. For instance, a character who is stubborn may be challenging to work with, but their stubbornness could also be the thing that motivates them to achieve their goals. Similarly, a character who is impulsive may make rash decisions, but they may also be courageous and willing to take risks that others wouldn't. By adding flaws to characters, it creates scenarios where they can face obstacles and challenges, which adds depth and complexity to their personalities.

Using flaws to create empathy and emotional resonance with readers

When characters have flaws, they face challenges that they must overcome, which can create a deep emotional connection between readers and the characters. This connection is strengthened when readers can see themselves in the character's struggle with a relatable flaw. Overcoming these flaws can inspire readers and make them feel connected to the character's journey.

29

Avoid stereotypes or cliches when creating characters of different races, genders, or sexual orientations.

Create characters that have many layers and avoid being too straightforward. One approach is to steer clear of common character stereotypes. For instance, the "damsel in distress" or the "strong, silent type" have been overused and tend to lack complexity.

Subverting and Challenging Typical Character Archetypes
You can make your characters more unique and interesting by adding a fresh perspective to traditional character archetypes. For instance, rather than sticking to the cliched "bad boy" persona, you could create a character who grapples with addiction and is striving to better their life. This brings depth to the character and avoids being too predictable.

Avoiding Predictable Character Development
To avoid creating predictable characters, you can surprise

readers by making your characters behave in unexpected ways. For instance, if you have a character who is typically logical and rational, you can make them act impulsively in certain situations. This unexpected behavior can add complexity and depth to the character.

Using Character Development to Break Free from Traditional Tropes

Developing your characters throughout the story can help them become more unique and multi-dimensional. By having them face challenges that force them to reexamine their values and beliefs, or by showing how their relationships with other characters affect their growth, they can break away from traditional character tropes and become more complex.

Creating Authentic and Respectful Diverse Characters

Create diverse characters that are authentic and respectful to research and understand the unique backgrounds and experiences of the characters you want to create. You should reflect their individual perspectives and identities in their personality, dialogue, and actions. Also, make sure to avoid stereotypes and assumptions about any specific group of people.

Pitfalls to Avoid When Writing Characters of Different Backgrounds

A common mistake to avoid is creating characters that are overly simplistic or stereotypical. Do thorough research and consult diverse perspectives when crafting characters from different backgrounds. Another trap to steer clear of is cultural appropriation, as it can be seen as insensitive or disrespectful.

Researching and Educating Yourself on Different Cultures and Communities

Create authentic characters from different cultures and communities, you can use various resources to educate yourself. This can include reading books, watching documentaries or films, and speaking with people who have firsthand experience with the culture or community you want to write about. Remember to approach your research with an open mind and a willingness to learn, and avoid relying on stereotypes or media representations.

Avoiding Harmful Stereotypes and Tropes in Character Creation

To avoid perpetuating harmful stereotypes or tropes, create characters that are multi-dimensional and not solely defined by their background or identity. Avoid using language that reinforces cliches or stereotypes and seek feedback from people who have firsthand experience with the culture or community you want to write about. Be open to making changes based on that feedback.

Using Diverse Characters to Enhance Your Story

When you create diverse characters in your story, you provide a more complete and nuanced view of the world. Different characters bring unique perspectives and experiences that make the story richer and more inclusive. This way, readers from various backgrounds can relate to the story. Diverse characters can also challenge common stereotypes and broaden readers' understanding of different cultures and communities.

30

Consider how your characters' conflicts and desires play off each other

Create conflicts that align with your characters' motivations and desires, and consider what each character wants and how their goals might oppose each other. Alternatively, think about the values that each character holds dear and how these values may come into conflict with one another. For instance, one character may value honesty while another places great importance on loyalty, which can lead to a conflict where one character must choose between revealing the truth and remaining faithful to the other character.

Conflict Examples: How Conflicts Drive the Story Forward

Conflicts that move the story forward are those that hold significance and influence the characters in some way. For instance, a conflict between the main character and their enemy that poses a danger to the character or their loved ones can create suspense and urgency that propels the story forward. Similarly, a conflict between two friends that jeopardizes their bond can evoke emotions in the reader and keep them engaged in the story.

Multi-Layered Conflicts: Involving Different Characters and Storylines

Create multi-layered conflicts, and consider how the conflicts and desires of different characters connect and interact with each other. You can also add external factors or events to complicate the conflicts. For instance, a sudden natural calamity or political unrest can bring additional challenges and conflicts for the characters to face.

Resolving Conflict: Ensuring Satisfying Resolutions

A resolution to a conflict that feels satisfying should make sense according to the personalities and motivations of the characters involved. It's essential to avoid an ending that seems too easy or coincidental. To achieve a satisfactory resolution, ensure that the characters take an active role in resolving the conflict instead of relying on outside forces to fix it.

Revealing Character: Using Conflict to Reveal New Aspects of Characters

Conflicts can help readers learn more about characters by challenging them and making them face their fears and biases. When characters go through tough situations, readers can see their true selves, what they believe in, and what motivates them. Moreover, conflicts can be a chance for characters to develop and transform, and readers can witness how their experiences shape them throughout the story.

31

Give your characters unique and memorable traits

Having unique and memorable traits makes characters that are captivating and stand out. Such characters are more likely to be memorable, making a lasting impression on readers even after they've finished reading the story.

Examples of Memorable Character Traits

There are many ways to create memorable character traits. They can include physical features, such as scars or unusual hair, personality quirks like a nervous tick or a sarcastic sense of humor. Other examples may include special skills or talents, particular hobbies or interests, or a distinct way of dressing or speaking.

Balancing Unique Traits and Realism in Character Development

Having too many unique traits can make a character seem unrealistic or exaggerated. Therefore, strike a balance between creating unique traits and making the character believable. This means that a character should have enough interesting features to make them memorable but not too many to make them seem like cartoon characters.

Using Character Traits to Drive the Plot

The unique traits of a character can significantly impact the plot and story development. Traits can influence a character's decisions and actions, which can impact the story's events. For instance, a character's strong desire to succeed might lead them to take risks and push themselves, while their sense of right and wrong might drive them to stand up against injustice.

Examples of quirks or mannerisms that can make a character stand out

Some things that make a character unique and memorable are their physical habits, unique phrases they use, interesting hobbies they have, and how they dress. These quirks can help to set them apart from other characters and make them stand out in the reader's mind.

Using character quirks to reveal personality traits or motivations

The unique quirks of a character can be used to show what they are like or what drives them. For instance, if a character tends to bite their nails when they are worried, it could indicate that they are anxious or uncertain. Similarly, if a character is often playing with a particular item, it could mean they have an emotional connection to it or need it for comfort.

Pitfalls to avoid when creating unique quirks or mannerisms

One mistake to avoid is making the quirk too extreme or

unrealistic, which can make the character appear silly or two-dimensional. Another is to rely too heavily on the quirk, which can create a character that lacks complexity or depth. Find a middle ground between a memorable quirk that sets the character apart, while also allowing them to be fully realized and multi-dimensional.

Ensuring consistency between character quirks and personality/backstory

To make sure that a character's quirks match their personality and backstory, consider their motivations and overall character development. Does the quirk align with the character's past experiences and current aspirations? Does it seem natural for the character to have developed such a quirk based on their personality traits and life journey? By addressing these questions, you can ensure that the character's quirks are consistent with their personality and help to flesh out their character.

32

Avoid cliched character archetypes

Using overused character archetypes in a story can make it feel dull and predictable. To make your story captivating, create distinctive and fascinating characters that will hook readers.

Common Character Archetypes to Avoid in Writing

Some character types that are overused and should be avoided include the helpless victim who needs to be rescued, the all-knowing mentor figure, the purely evil antagonist, and the stereotypical popular athlete or cheerleader. These types have been used so often that they lack originality and can make your story feel uninteresting.

Balancing Uniqueness and Archetypes in Character Creation

To make a character stand out from an archetype, you can add some unique or surprising qualities to them. For instance, your protagonist might have a flaw that is not typical of heroes, such as being afraid of heights or having a habit of putting things off. This can make them more intriguing and relatable to readers.

Subverting Archetypes for Unique Character Development

You can make a character more interesting by taking a commonly used archetype and giving it a new twist. For instance, a villain with a tragic past or a mentor who has their own flaws and secrets can make for a more intricate and captivating character.

Examples of Cliched Characters in Literature and Film

Some overused and predictable characters are the helpless woman who needs saving in fairy tales, the elderly and wise teacher in Star Wars, the cruel and jealous stepmother in Cinderella, and the popular and athletic high school students in teen movies. These character archetypes are so common that they no longer surprise or engage readers or viewers.

Identifying and Avoiding Cliched Characters During the Writing Process

To avoid cliched characters, you can do some research on character archetypes and then come up with new and unique ideas for your characters. Get feedback from beta readers or other writers to make sure your characters are not too predictable. And, to make your characters feel more real, be sure to give them flaws and complexities.

33

Use dialogue to reveal character traits and personalities

Using dialogue shows the personalities and relationships of characters in your story. You can reveal a character's personality by the way they speak, such as in a hesitant or confident tone. Additionally, the relationships between characters can be shown through the tone and choice of words in their dialogue. For example, a tense relationship might be characterized by curt or sarcastic remarks, while a close relationship might be revealed through inside jokes or shared experiences.

Writing Realistic and Natural Dialogue

To write dialogue that sounds realistic, you can observe how people talk in real life and listen to their phrasing, word choice, and tone. Another tip is to read the dialogue out loud to ensure it flows naturally. You can also add contractions and interruptions to make the dialogue feel authentic.

How a Character's Speech Patterns Reflect their Personality

The way a character talks can give insights into their personality. For instance, a well-educated character might use long sentences and big words while a less-educated one may use shorter and simpler sentences. A character who is shy may talk in a more hesitant way compared to a confident character who may speak more assertively.

Using Body Language and Nonverbal Cues to Reveal Character Traits

Sometimes, a character's body language and nonverbal cues can provide more information about their personality than what they say. For instance, a character who avoids eye contact may be concealing something, while a character who fidgets may feel nervous or anxious. You can also use facial expressions, gestures, and posture to communicate a character's emotions and personality.

How Dialogue between Two Characters Reveals Both of their Personalities

When two characters have a conversation, it can tell us a lot about their personalities and relationship. For instance, two friends talking may sound easygoing and relaxed with lots of shared memories and jokes. However, a conversation between two enemies could sound tense and may have several sarcastic remarks. Through dialogue, you can also show how characters respond to one another, revealing more about their personalities.

Using Dialogue to Create Tension Between Characters

Create tension between characters through dialogue by making characters with opposing goals or beliefs talk to each other. This can lead to arguments or debates that heighten the conflict between them. Another way is to use subtext, where the characters say one thing but mean another, which can create tension as the reader knows that there is something deeper going on beneath the surface.

Examples of Dialogue That Can Reveal Hidden Agendas or Ulterior Motives

For instance, a character may appear to be saying something harmless or ordinary, but readers can sense that their real intention is to control or deceive the other character. Similarly, a character may use flattering or kind words to achieve their own goals, revealing their hidden agenda.

Using Dialogue to Build Intimacy or Distance Between Characters

To build a sense of closeness between characters, dialogue can include references to shared experiences and inside jokes that only they would understand. Alternatively, using short, abrupt phrases or sentences can create a sense of distance and tension. By using subtle language cues and subtext, you can create an emotional distance that intensifies the conflict.

34

Use character interactions to reveal conflict and tension

To create tension and conflict between characters, you can use dialogue and nonverbal cues like body language and facial expressions. Each character should have their own way of speaking, and their interactions with other characters should be filled with tension and hidden motives. This adds depth and complexity to your story and keeps readers engaged.

Examples of Interpersonal Conflicts That Can Drive a Story Forward

Conflicts between characters can stem from various reasons, like differing beliefs, values, or goals. For instance, in "The Great Gatsby" by F. Scott Fitzgerald, the disagreement between the main character and his love interest Daisy is caused by their different social standings and conflicting wants. This disagreement moves the story ahead and generates tension between them.

Using Character Interactions to Build Suspense

Create suspense in your story by using character interactions to reveal information slowly and in a subtle way. One way to do this is by having characters keep secrets from each other or lie to each other, which can create tension and make readers curious about what will happen next. Another way is to use dialogue to hint at future events, which can create a feeling of anticipation and foreshadowing.

Revealing New Information About Your Characters Through Interactions

To make your story engaging, your characters should interact with each other in ways that reveal new information about themselves. For example, you can use dialogue to show a character's motivations, backstory, or secrets, or you can show how they react in certain situations. This will help to deepen their personalities and make your story more interesting for your readers.

35

Consider how your characters' relationships with each other change over the course of the story

To show how a relationship between characters changes over time, focus on important moments or events that affect their bond. For example, if two characters initially don't know each other well but later become good friends, you can depict how they grow closer through shared experiences and by sharing personal information. Additionally, you can demonstrate how their interactions change over time, including how they communicate and their body language towards each other.

Factors Affecting Character Relationships

There are many things that can impact how characters interact with each other. Their unique personalities, beliefs, and values can either work well together or cause conflict. The situation or location in which they meet can also have an effect. Furthermore, their past history and experiences with one another can heavily influence their current relationship.

How Interactions with One Character can Affect a Character's Relationship with Another

A character's interactions with one person can influence their relationship with another character. This can happen when two people have different opinions or goals. For instance, if a character starts dating someone new, their best friend may feel left out or envious, which can create conflict in their relationship. Similarly, if a character befriends someone that their friend doesn't like, this can cause a disagreement between them.

Relationships that Drive Plot: Examples and Techniques

Relationships play a vital role in driving the plot of a story forward. The type of relationship depends on the genre and tone of the story. For example, a romantic relationship can create tension and obstacles that the characters must overcome. A mentor-protégé relationship can lead to personal growth and development. Other relationships that can drive the plot forward include rivalries, friendships that are tested by external factors, and strained family relationships due to conflicts or secrets. The relationships that you choose to focus on should be relevant to the story you want to tell.

Examples of Relationships that Undergo Significant Changes in a Story

Different kinds of relationships can change a lot over time. For instance, a romantic relationship might begin well but become weaker later due to problems from inside or outside. A strong friendship could be broken due to a betrayal or disagreement. Sometimes, family relationships become tense because of secrets, misunderstandings or distance. By portraying various relationships in your story, you can make it richer and more complex.

Creating Realistic and Layered Character Relationships

Writing a captivating story creates realistic and complex relationships between characters. This can be done by exploring the personalities, backgrounds, and motivations of each character and understanding how they interact with one another. By revealing each character's backstory, personality traits, and worldview, you can create a more nuanced and authentic relationship. Additionally, showing the characters' vulnerabilities and flaws can add depth to the relationship, making it more relatable to readers.

Avoiding One-Dimensional Relationships: Tips and Strategies

To avoid creating flat and predictable relationships, give each character their own unique motivations and goals that may not always align with the others. This will create tension and complexity within the relationship. Show the characters interacting in different settings and situations to allow their relationship to grow and change over time. Avoid relying on overused cliches or stereotypes and instead focus on creating authentic and interesting dynamics between the characters.

Creating Tension and Conflict in Character Relationships

To add tension and conflict in character relationships, think about what each character wants and what their goals are. If two characters have different goals, it can create natural tension that moves the story forward. Also, adding secrets or hidden motives can create a sense of betrayal or mistrust that makes the relationship more complicated. Additionally, think about how outside factors or events may influence the relationship, like having the characters work together on an important project. By adding moments of tension and conflict, you can make the relationship more interesting and engaging.

Using Relationships to Show Growth and Development in the Story

Character relationships can help demonstrate how characters grow and change throughout the story. One way to do this is to show a relationship that starts off negative, but becomes more positive as the characters evolve. This can create a sense of closure and resolution. Another way to show growth is to have characters learn from each other, which can happen in mentor-protégé relationships. The mentor can teach the protégé, while the protégé can challenge the mentor's beliefs. This can show how the characters have developed as the story progresses.

36

Consider character goals and motivations and how they drive the plot

Having clear and convincing character motivations helps explain why characters act and make certain decisions. If a character's motivations are not well-defined or convincing, they may appear boring or unappealing.

How Character Motivations can Drive the Plot

When characters in a story have different motivations, it can create tension and conflict that push the plot forward. For instance, if a character is driven by a desire for revenge, their actions and decisions will be affected by that motivation, leading to clashes with other characters and driving the story towards a resolution or a confrontation.

The Possibility of Character Motivations Changing Throughout the Story

A character's motivations can evolve and transform

throughout the story, as they encounter new situations and undergo personal growth. This can make the character more dynamic and interesting, and can also create new possibilities for conflicts and plot twists.

Examples of Stories Where Character Motivations Drive the Plot

In "The Count of Monte Cristo" by Alexandre Dumas, the protagonist's desire for revenge is the main driving force of the plot. Similarly, in "Gone Girl" by Gillian Flynn, the motivations of the two main characters are what propel the story towards an unexpected and intense ending.

Using Character Motivations to Create Conflict and Tension in a Story

When characters have different and opposing motivations, it can cause tension and conflict between them. For instance, if one character is motivated by love and another by greed, their motivations can clash and create tension that drives the plot forward. Similarly, by keeping a character's motivation hidden or unclear, the reader is left in suspense and tension as they try to unravel the character's true intentions.

Creating Compelling Goals and Motivations for Characters

To create effective goals, you should think about what your character desires and why they desire it. This could be something tangible, like a job or an object, or it could be something intangible, like love or inner peace. Once you have established your character's goal, consider what motivates them to pursue it, such as a sense of duty, a desire for power, or a need for validation.

The Impact of Character Goals and Motivations on Relationships

When two characters have different goals or reasons for doing something, it can cause disagreements and problems between them. For instance, if one character is trying to get a job that another character is interested in, it can create feelings of envy or rivalry. On the other hand, if two characters are striving for the same goal but have different motives, they might have a disagreement about the best approach to take. By incorporating these conflicts, you can add excitement and suspense to your story.

Always keep in mind that the goals and motivations of your characters are the fuel that propels your story forward. Take the time to fully develop them and consider how they can affect your plot and your characters' relationships. Best of luck with your writing!

37

Avoid creating characters that are too similar to each other or to yourself.

To make your characters stand out, give them special qualities like a unique speaking style, a distinct sense of humor, or specific talents. Additionally, creating characters with different backgrounds, beliefs, and values can influence their perspectives and behavior in the story.

Ways to Differentiate Characters' Voices and Motivations

To differentiate characters' voices and motivations, you can make them speak and act differently from each other. This can be achieved by giving each character unique dialogue patterns, speech mannerisms, and goals. Each character can also have different values and priorities, which can affect how they make decisions and react to conflicts and relationships.

Common Mistakes to Avoid When Creating Similar Characters

One thing to avoid is giving characters similar speech patterns and dialogue styles. This can make them sound too similar and interchangeable. Another mistake to avoid is creating characters with identical motivations and goals, as this can make them less interesting and reduce the potential for conflict.

Ensuring Each Character has a Unique Perspective and World-view

To ensure that each character has a unique perspective and worldview, create characters with different backgrounds, experiences, and beliefs. Additionally, you can take into account how each character's personality and motivations shape their perception of the world and their relationships with other characters.

Using Character Relationships to Highlight Differences and Similarities

Character relationships can be a useful tool to showcase differences and similarities in personalities, values, and motivations. When characters have opposing values, they may come into conflict, while characters with similar motivations may form close bonds. These relationships can also serve as opportunities for characters to learn from each other and grow, ultimately shaping the course of the story.

38

Show, don't tell, when it comes to character traits

"Show, don't tell" is a common advice for writers, which means that instead of plainly telling the reader about a character's traits or emotions, you should illustrate those traits or emotions through their actions, dialogue, and description.

How to Show a Character's Traits Instead of Telling

To show a character's traits, you can use descriptive language that portrays their actions or appearance. For instance, instead of stating "He was angry," you can write about him clenching his fists or raising his voice. Additionally, using dialogue can help display character traits by having them say things that reflect their personality.

Example of "Telling" versus "Showing" in Writing

Instead of simply stating a character's traits, you can demonstrate those traits through their actions and behavior. For instance, instead of saying that a character is honest, you can show them telling the truth even when it's difficult or inconvenient. By doing this, you help the reader to experience the character's personality traits firsthand and create a more engaging and immersive reading experience.

How "Showing" a Character's Traits Makes Them More Relatable

When you show a character's traits through their actions and behavior, readers can relate to them better and they become more believable. This can create an emotional bond between the reader and the character, making them more memorable.

Using Both "Showing" and "Telling" to Reveal Character Traits

While there are instances where "telling" might be required to convey certain elements of the story or character, it's generally advisable to use "showing" to reveal character traits through actions and behaviors. This helps to create a more lively and captivating narrative that can resonate with the readers.

39

Use character arcs to show how your characters change and grow throughout the story.

A character arc is a path that a character takes during a story, which can involve changes in their personality, beliefs, or actions. It helps readers see how the character develops and changes as the story unfolds, which can make them feel more connected to the character on an emotional level.

Using a Character's Arc to Drive the Plot Forward

A character's journey can be used to move the story forward by introducing obstacles and challenges that they must overcome. As the character develops and evolves, their choices and actions can have a significant impact on the plot and determine the story's outcome.

Examples of Character Arcs that Show Growth and Development

There are different types of character arcs that display

growth and progress. A character may overcome their fears or weaknesses, develop empathy, or make peace with their past. For example, in "To Kill a Mockingbird" by Harper Lee, Scout Finch learns about the harsh realities of racism and injustice and becomes a more compassionate and understanding person, moving from naivety and innocence to maturity.

Ensuring Consistency in a Character's Arc with their Personality and Motivations

To make sure that a character's arc makes sense, establish their personality and motivations early on in the story. This way, you can stay true to their character traits as their arc progresses. The character's growth should stem from their core values and beliefs, and the challenges they face should challenge and complicate those beliefs in a believable way.

Using Character Arcs to Create a Satisfying and Meaningful Story

Character arcs can help create a satisfying and meaningful story by providing readers with a sense of closure and resolution as the character progresses and overcomes challenges. This allows readers to connect with the character on an emotional level and can leave them feeling inspired or moved. A well-executed character arc can make a story more memorable and enjoyable to read, as readers become invested in the character's journey and want to see how it all turns out.

III

Plotting And Story Structure

40

Develop a clear and compelling plot

The main character's journey is important in any story. As the plot unfolds, the main character should face obstacles and challenges that make them grow and change. These challenges could be physical or emotional or both. The character should learn and acquire new skills or perspectives that help them overcome the main conflict and achieve their goals.

Driving the Plot Forward: Understanding the Main Conflict

The main conflict is what moves the story forward. It's the problem that the main character must solve and should be presented early in the story. The problem can come from outside, like a fight against a villain or a disaster, or from within, like a battle with addiction or mental illness. Whatever it is, it should be captivating and drive the main character to act.

The Changing Stakes of the Story: How They Impact the Plot

The stakes in a story are what the main character has to gain or lose as they try to achieve their goals. They need to be important and create a feeling of urgency for the main character to succeed. As the story progresses, the stakes should get even higher, making the situation more urgent and the consequences of failure more severe. This can create excitement and keep readers interested in the story.

The Contribution of Secondary Characters to the Plot

Supporting characters are significant in any story. They help to shape the protagonist's character, add humor, and even become friends or foes. It is essential to ensure that each supporting character has a reason to be in the story, and that their actions contribute to the main plot. Each character should have their own distinct personality and reasons for acting, and they should have a significant interaction with the protagonist.

The Impact of Setting on the Plot and its Development

The setting of a story affects the plot in various ways. It can establish the mood and atmosphere of the story and present challenges for the protagonist to overcome. It should be described in detail to help readers imagine the world of the story. The setting can create tension and contribute to the plot by presenting obstacles or hazards for the protagonist to face. For instance, a story set in a dark forest might include dangerous creatures and treacherous paths that the protagonist must navigate to reach their goal.

Always keep in mind that crafting an engaging plot requires dedication and hard work. By taking the time to plan and paying attention to the details, you can create a story that will capture your audience's imagination and keep them hooked until the end.

41

Use a clear narrative arc with a beginning, middle, and end:

A narrative arc is the backbone of your story, providing a structure for its development. It consists of three parts - the beginning, middle, and end - and is essential for creating a satisfying and cohesive story. The start sets up the characters and setting, introduces the problem, and establishes what's at stake. The middle is where most of the action happens, with characters facing increasing challenges and obstacles as they strive to resolve the conflict. Finally, the end brings closure as the conflict is resolved, and the characters undergo a transformation.

Crafting a Clear Narrative Arc: Tips and Techniques

To make sure that your story follows a clear narrative arc, plan it out in advance. This involves creating an outline that maps out the beginning, middle, and end of your story and identifying key events and plot points that will occur in each section. By referring to your outline as you write, you can ensure that your story stays on track and maintains a cohesive structure.

Key events that shape the rising action of the story

The rising action is where things start to get more exciting and the tension builds up. It's where the protagonist encounters challenges and difficulties that must be overcome in order to reach their goals. This phase may also have moments of setbacks or difficulties that make the protagonist's task even harder. The goal is to build up to a climax that will resolve the central conflict of the story.

The climax: how it differs from the rest of the narrative

The climax is the most intense moment in the story, where the main conflict is finally resolved. It's different from the rest of the story because it's the result of everything that has happened so far. The protagonist must face their greatest challenge, and the way they handle it will determine the outcome of the story. The climax is usually a dramatic and unforgettable event that sticks with the reader.

Major turning points and their impact on the plot

Major turning points in a story are moments when something important happens that change the direction of the narrative. The protagonist might face a new challenge, make a crucial decision, or experience a significant event. These turning points can have positive or negative effects on the story and can influence how the protagonist moves forward. They help to keep the story engaging and interesting while driving the plot forward.

The reflection of the narrative arc in the resolution of the

story

The end of the story is called the resolution, where the protagonist's journey comes to a close, and the central problem is solved. This part of the story should be satisfying, wrapping up any loose ends and providing a sense of closure. The resolution should also reflect the overall story, with the protagonist achieving their goals and undergoing growth or change. This conclusion should leave the reader feeling content and fulfilled.

Benefits of using a story arc to structure a novel

Structuring your novel using a story arc can have many benefits. It provides a clear direction and purpose for the story, ensuring that the plot moves forward in an engaging and logical way. It also helps to build tension and suspense, leading to a satisfying and exciting climax. Ultimately, it creates a cohesive and fulfilling story that leaves readers feeling satisfied.

Keep in mind that structuring your novel with a story arc is only one way of doing it. However, it can be an effective tool to ensure that your story flows logically and captivates readers. By planning and paying close attention to details, you can create a compelling narrative that keeps readers engaged throughout the entire story.

Avoiding Common Mistakes in Structuring a Narrative Arc

A common mistake is taking too long to get to the action or main conflict of the story, which can bore readers. Another mistake is having too many different storylines or subplots that can confuse the reader. Make sure that every event in your story serves a purpose and advances the narrative arc, rather than being irrelevant. Lastly, give your story a resolution that is both satisfying and meaningful.

Ensuring Every Element Contributes to the Narrative Arc

Make sure that every element in your story, such as characters and plot, contributes to the overall narrative arc. You can do this by considering how the actions and decisions of your characters fit into the arc of the story. Similarly, each plot point should either build tension or resolve conflict to contribute to the overall narrative arc. By keeping the narrative arc in mind as you develop each element of your story, you can create a more cohesive and satisfying whole.

Examples of Novels with Strong Narrative Arcs

Some examples of novels with a strong narrative arc are "To Kill a Mockingbird" by Harper Lee, "The Great Gatsby" by F. Scott Fitzgerald, and "The Catcher in the Rye" by J.D. Salinger. Each of these books has a clear narrative arc with a beginning, middle, and end, which creates tension and resolves conflicts in an enjoyable way.

42

Create tension and conflict to keep readers engaged

In a story, the protagonist and antagonist should have different goals and desires that clash with each other. This creates tension and moves the story along. The protagonist wants something that the antagonist is trying to stop or obtain, and this back-and-forth creates excitement and keeps the reader engaged. The bigger the difference in goals, the greater the conflict and suspense.

Overcoming internal conflicts

A character's inner struggles or conflicts play a crucial role in their growth and development in the story. These internal battles could stem from personal flaws or doubts that the character must confront to achieve their objectives. Such conflicts could include self-doubt, guilt, or fear, and they should align with the character's overarching story. Overcoming these obstacles is equally as significant as overcoming external challenges, and they add depth and relatability to the character's journey.

Facing external conflicts

External conflicts are the challenges that the protagonist faces to reach their goals. These challenges could be physical obstacles or more abstract issues, such as navigating a tricky political landscape. The protagonist must overcome these obstacles, and this creates tension and pushes the story forward.

Contribution of conflicts to character development

Conflicts are significant for character development because they challenge the protagonist and help them grow throughout the story. Every conflict that the protagonist encounters should test their abilities, forcing them to learn and adapt to new situations. At the end of the story, the protagonist should have transformed in some way, having learned valuable lessons from their experiences.

Building tension through storytelling techniques

Tension is an important element in a story and it increases as the protagonist encounters more challenging obstacles. The tension can be created through different techniques such as gradually increasing the level of difficulty in the challenges faced by the protagonist, hinting at future conflicts, or using sensory details to make the reader feel as if they are in the midst of the action.

Don't forget that conflict and tension are key ingredients for keeping your readers interested and invested in your story. By thoughtfully creating conflicts and gradually increasing the tension, you can craft a captivating narrative that will leave your readers excited and engaged until the very end.

43

Use foreshadowing to hint at future events and create tension

Foreshadowing is a writing technique that drops hints about what might happen in your story in the future. It can help keep readers engaged by building up tension and excitement. By weaving in small clues and suggestions throughout your story, you can create an atmosphere of suspense and keep your readers guessing what might happen next.

Examples of foreshadowing in the novel and their impact on the plot

Foreshadowing can be done in many ways, such as dropping subtle clues or making more obvious references. For instance, a character's recurring dream might foreshadow what will happen later in the story, or a seemingly insignificant object might be mentioned multiple times before becoming important. Foreshadowing can affect the plot in a big way by creating a feeling of inevitability and increasing tension as the story unfolds.

Reader reactions to foreshadowing and its effectiveness as a storytelling technique

Foreshadowing is generally well-received by readers as it makes the story more thrilling and engaging. It also helps the readers to become more invested in the story by encouraging them to think about what could happen next. Foreshadowing is a powerful storytelling tool as it enables authors to create tension, depth and complexity in their narrative.

Potential drawbacks of using foreshadowing in a story

Using too much or too obvious foreshadowing can spoil the story's impact. Finding the right balance is important because too much can make the story predictable, while too little can make the ending feel incomplete.

Strategies for effectively using foreshadowing without revealing too much of the plot

To effectively use foreshadowing, an author must balance the amount of information provided to readers to build anticipation without revealing too much of the plot. This can be achieved by using subtle hints that only become significant later or misdirection to throw readers off. The author must be strategic and intentional in their use of foreshadowing to enhance the story and not detract from it.

The Art of Foreshadowing: Balancing Hint and Suspense

Be subtle when using foreshadowing in your story. You don't want to give away too much information, but instead, provide enough clues to keep your readers interested. You can achieve this by using symbols or imagery to hint at what's to come. Alternatively, you can use dialogue to give a hint without revealing too much.

Types of Foreshadowing: Enhancing Tension and Plot

There are various types of foreshadowing that can create tension in your story. For instance, you can use "Chekhov's Gun" by introducing an object that appears insignificant at the beginning but later becomes significant. You can also use "flashforward" to show a future event that hints at what's to come. Both these methods are effective in keeping readers engaged and creating a sense of anticipation.

Learning From the Best: Effective Foreshadowing in Well-Known Novels

In "The Great Gatsby" by F. Scott Fitzgerald, the green light shining on the other side of the water represents Gatsby's desire for Daisy and hints at the tragedy that occurs later in the story. In "Harry Potter and the Sorcerer's Stone" by J.K. Rowling, the mysterious person on the motorcycle at the start of the book is later revealed to be an important character. In "The Hunger Games" by Suzanne Collins, the Mockingjay pin that Katniss wears early on symbolizes her defiance and plays a critical role in the plot later in the story.

44

Use flashbacks to add depth and complexity to your story.

Flashbacks are a useful way to give readers more insight into a character's backstory or reveal important information that happened before the main events of the story. However, use them wisely and only when they add value to the current plot.

Common Mistakes to Avoid When Using Flashbacks in Writing

A common mistake writers make when using flashbacks is using them too often or at the wrong moments in the story. This can affect the flow of the story and make it confusing for readers. Additionally, some writers may use flashbacks to reveal information that could have been presented in the present time frame, making the flashback seem unnecessary. It's essential to ensure that the flashback is smoothly incorporated into the story and doesn't feel like an abrupt or disjointed interruption.

Balancing Flashbacks and Foreshadowing in Writing With-

out Disrupting Pacing

Using flashbacks and foreshadowing in moderation and at the right moments maintains the flow of the story. Flashbacks should only be used when they contribute to the plot and are necessary while foreshadowing should be subtly incorporated into the story. Smooth transitions between the present timeline, flashbacks, and foreshadowing can help to prevent abrupt interruptions to the reader's experience.

45

Plan your plot twists carefully to avoid predictability

Plot twists are an important part of a good story, but they can be difficult to execute without feeling forced or expected. One way to avoid this is by leaving subtle clues throughout the story that make the twist feel natural and earned, rather than sudden and unbelievable

Example of Effective Planning for Plot Twists

Imagine you are writing a mystery story and you want to surprise your readers by revealing that the protagonist's friend, who they thought was innocent, is actually the mastermind behind the crime. To achieve this, you can drop small clues throughout the story that hints at the friend's true motives. For example, you can add comments or actions that seem insignificant at first but will become significant once the twist is revealed. The idea is to make the clues subtle enough that readers won't immediately catch on, but significant enough that they will make sense when the twist is revealed.

Common Types of Plot Twists in Stories

There are several types of plot twists that writers commonly use, such as the unreliable narrator, mistaken identity, and hidden past. However, use these twists carefully and do not rely on them too heavily, as they can become predictable and lose their impact.

The Impact of Plot Twists on Character Development and Reader Engagement

Plot twists can be a powerful tool for developing characters by throwing unexpected challenges at them, leading to revealing new aspects of their personalities. Moreover, a well-planned plot twist can maintain the reader's interest by introducing uncertainty and anticipation. However, an author should use them strategically, ensuring they serve a purpose in the story, rather than relying on them to cover up for a weak plot.

Example of a Story that Uses Plot Twists Effectively

A great example of a story that has effectively used plot twists is "Gone Girl" by Gillian Flynn. The book has multiple surprising moments that maintain the reader's curiosity until the very end, and each of these moments has been subtly hinted at throughout the story. These plot twists not only progress the plot but also uncover new aspects of the characters and their reasons.

46

Use cliffhangers and Plot twists to keep readers hooked

Cliffhangers can be really effective at making readers want to keep reading your book. But make sure that they're not just there for show. Each cliffhanger should leave the reader with a question or sense of excitement that will keep them engaged and curious about what will happen next.

Avoiding Overused or Predictable Cliffhangers

To steer clear of using unoriginal cliffhangers, you should try to be creative and think of fresh and surprising ways to keep your readers engaged. Moreover, use cliffhangers in moderation so that they don't become monotonous or contrived.

How Cliffhangers Contribute to Emotional Engagement

Cliffhangers can make a story more exciting and keep readers interested. They can build up tension and suspense, making the reader feel emotionally invested in the story. They can also create a sense of danger or urgency, making the story more exciting and engaging.

Potential Drawbacks of Using Cliffhangers in a Novel

Although cliffhangers can be a useful tool in storytelling, use them thoughtfully. If they're used too often or not done well, they can backfire and make the story feel forced or contrived. Readers may also become frustrated if the cliffhanger leaves too many unanswered questions or doesn't deliver on the anticipated resolution. Therefore, use cliffhangers judiciously and ensure they serve the story in a meaningful way.

Common Types of Cliffhangers Used in Novels

Authors use various types of cliffhangers to maintain readers' interest in the story. Some of the common cliffhangers include leaving a character in a perilous situation, ending a chapter with a surprising revelation or twist, or leaving an important question unanswered. However, it's essential to use cliffhangers thoughtfully, and not too frequently, as they might become predictable or lose their effectiveness.

Building Suspense Leading up to a Cliffhanger: Tips for Authors

To keep readers on edge and build suspense leading up to a cliffhanger, an author should create a sense of tension or urgency in the scene. This can be done by using pacing, dialogue, or descriptive language that emphasizes the importance of the situation. Foreshadowing can also be used to hint at a future event or reveal that will be resolved in the cliffhanger. However, balance this information carefully and do not give away too much too soon, as it can reduce the impact of the cliffhanger.

Examples of Novels That Use Cliffhangers or Suspenseful Chapter Endings Effectively

An example of a book that uses cliffhangers effectively is "Gone Girl" by Gillian Flynn, where each chapter ends with a new revelation or twist that keeps the reader hooked. Another example is "The Hunger Games" by Suzanne Collins, where cliffhangers are used to create tension and danger, with each chapter ending with a new challenge for the main character to face, keeping the reader engaged and interested in the story.

Understanding the Difference between Cliffhangers and Plot Twists

Cliffhangers and plot twists are great tools to keep readers engaged in a story. A cliffhanger is a moment in the story where the reader is left hanging at a critical point, usually at the end of a chapter or section, to keep them guessing and wondering. Whereas a plot twist is a sudden and unexpected turn in the story that changes the reader's understanding of what's happening, which could be a significant turning point or a small revelation that alters the reader's perception of the characters or situations.

How Plot Twists Impact Pacing and Emotional Engagement

When a plot twist is well-done, it can greatly affect the pacing and emotional connection of the reader. It can add a fresh dose of excitement to the story, making the reader more alert and encouraging them to rethink their previous assumptions about the plot and characters. The plot twist can generate more anxiety and suspense, causing the reader to feel more eager to know what comes next.

Common Types of Plot Twists in Novels

Authors can use various types of plot twists to engage and surprise readers. Some of the most common ones include identity twists, betrayal twists, revelation twists, and turnabout twists. For example, an identity twist can happen when a character is revealed to be someone other than who they claimed to be, while a revelation twist occurs when new information is unveiled that changes the reader's understanding of the plot or characters. However, these are just a few examples, and there are many more ways to use plot twists in a story.

Examples of Novels that Use Plot Twists Effectively

There are many examples of novels and movies that use plot twists effectively. For instance, "Gone Girl" by Gillian Flynn has a lot of surprises that keep readers engaged till the end. "The Sixth Sense" directed by M. Night Shyamalan is another great example where the plot twist at the end changes the whole story's perspective. "The Girl on the Train" by Paula Hawkins is a recent thriller book that uses plot twists to create suspense and keep the readers hooked.

<h1 style="text-align:center">47</h1>

Avoid cliched plot twists and consider multiple possible outcomes for key events

It's best to avoid clichéd plot twists that readers have come to expect, like the "it was all a dream," "hero's best friend is the villain," or "resurrection from the dead" twists. These have been overused and can make your writing predictable and uninteresting. Instead, try to create unique and surprising twists that fit your story and characters. Consider your characters' motivations and use them to create unexpected turns that make sense within the context of the story.

Creating Unique and Authentic Plot Twists: Tips for Authors

To avoid predictable plot twists, authors can be creative by doing something unexpected that defies reader expectations. They can also use the characters' personalities and goals to influence the plot twists. Additionally, authors can draw inspiration from real-life events or different story genres to create unique plot twists that are relevant to their stories. With imagination and originality, authors can create plot twists that are both surprising and authentic to their narrative.

Considering Multiple Outcomes: Benefits and Strategies for Avoiding Predictability

Thinking about different possible outcomes for key events in the story can help keep readers interested and engaged by creating a sense of suspense and uncertainty. It also allows the author to choose the best option for the story by carefully considering each possibility and selecting the one that is most engaging and authentic.

48

Consider using multiple POVs or timelines to add complexity to the story

When a story uses multiple points of view or timelines, it can become more interesting and complex. This is because the reader can see things from different angles, which can be exciting. Also, this can give the reader more information about the story's world, as different characters may know different things.

Common challenges faced by authors using multiple POVs or timelines

One of the main difficulties in using multiple POVs or timelines is to make sure they fit together and contribute to the story's overall purpose. Additionally, it can be challenging to keep each character distinct and maintain a consistent voice for them. Furthermore, presenting different timelines out of order can lead to confusion for readers.

Effectively managing multiple POVs or timelines to prevent confusion for the reader

To avoid confusing readers when using multiple POVs or timelines, authors should clearly identify each section or chapter with the character or timeline it is focused on. They should also establish each character's unique voice and perspective early on. Additionally, authors should ensure that each POV or timeline contributes something meaningful to the story, and not just add complexity for the sake of it.

Examples of novels that use multiple POVs or timelines effectively

"Cloud Atlas" by David Mitchell is a novel that combines six different stories that take place in various time periods and genres. Each story has a distinct point of view and is thematically connected to the others. Another example is "A Song of Ice and Fire" by George R.R. Martin, which uses multiple characters' points of view to tell a complex and layered story set in a vast, fantastical world.

Appropriate times to use multiple POVs or timelines in a novel

Multiple POVs or timelines can work well in different types of stories, but they're especially popular in literary fiction, historical fiction, and epic fantasy. They can help to make a story feel richer and more detailed, especially when there are many different storylines or ideas. But use them only when it makes sense for the story, not just to make things more complicated for the sake of it.

49

Be mindful of pacing – too much action or too little can turn readers off:

The pace of a story impacts how much the reader is emotionally invested in it. If the story is too slow, the reader might get bored, and if it's too fast, the reader might get overwhelmed. A perfect balance between the two will create an engaging and enjoyable reading experience.

Techniques for Controlling Pacing in a Story

Authors use several techniques to control the pacing of their stories. For example, they can vary the length of chapters to create a faster or slower pace. They can also use cliffhangers, plot twists, and dialogue to keep readers engaged and interested.

The Relationship Between Chapter Length and Pacing

The length of a chapter can affect the pacing of a story. Shorter chapters can make the story seem faster because they make readers curious about what will happen next. On the other hand, longer chapters can make the story seem slower by giving more time for character development and the story explanation. However, chapter length is not the only factor that impacts pacing, and an author can create a fast-paced story with longer chapters or a slower-paced story with shorter chapters.

Balancing Fast-Paced and Slow-Paced Sections of a Novel

To create a well-balanced story, an author must find the perfect pace for each section of their novel. The start of the book must be exciting to keep the reader interested, the middle section should have a slower pace for character and plot development, but still, keep the reader engaged, and the end of the book should speed up again as it builds towards the conclusion. By finding the right pace, an author can ensure that their readers will be emotionally invested in the story from beginning to end.

Another way to balance the pace of a story is by switching between fast-paced and slow-paced sections. This means that after an intense and thrilling scene, there can be a calmer and more thoughtful one. This balance can also contribute to creating a more engaging and fulfilling experience for the reader.

The Connection Between Pacing and Tension in a Story

Pacing and tension go hand in hand when it comes to keeping readers engaged emotionally. Tension comes from uncertainty, conflict, and suspense, while pacing affects how that tension is released. For instance, a slow pace can build tension by stretching out a suspenseful scene, while a fast pace can ease tension by providing an answer. Knowing this, an author can use pacing to improve the tension and emotional intensity of their story.

Tips for Maintaining a Consistent Pace in Your Novel

Pacing can impact the reader's experience. Here are some tips to help you maintain a consistent pace:

1. Plan your story: Before you start writing, plan your story and divide it into sections or chapters. This can help you understand how the story will progress and where to adjust the pace.
2. Use different sentence lengths: Varying sentence lengths is an effective way to control the pace. Shorter sentences quicken the pace, while longer ones slow it down.
3. Incorporate action and dialogue: Action and dialogue can help you maintain a consistent pace. They keep the story moving and engage readers with the characters.
4. Avoid unnecessary details: Don't include unnecessary details that can slow down the story's pace. Only include relevant information

Using Pacing to Build Tension and Keep the Reader Engaged

Pacing can make a story more interesting by keeping readers engaged. Here are a few ways to do that:

1. Use shorter sentences during action scenes or intense moments to create a sense of speed.
2. Slow the pace during calmer scenes to give readers a chance to catch their breath and focus on important details.
3. Keep readers interested with cliffhangers or surprises that make them want to keep reading.

4. Control the pace by varying the intensity of the action. You can start with a slow build-up, followed by a sudden burst of action, and then a brief pause before the tension builds again.

Common Pacing Mistakes and How to Avoid Them

One mistake writers make is having too many backstories or action scenes that make the story move too slowly or too quickly. To avoid these mistakes, writers should balance their scenes and make sure each one contributes to the story's pace. They should aim to keep the story moving consistently and smoothly.

Creating Urgency and Driving the Plot Forward: How Pacing Can Help

To make the story more exciting and interesting, pacing can be used to create a sense of urgency and tension. This can be done by using short sentences and paragraphs during intense moments, speeding up the action scenes, and building up suspense through dialogue and character actions.

50

Use symbolism and motifs to tie different parts of your story together

Symbolism is a strong technique that can give your story more significance and importance. You can use symbolism by giving objects, actions, or events a deeper meaning than their usual definition. For instance, a red rose can represent love or passion, while a dark and stormy night can signify danger or uncertainty. By using these symbols consistently in your story, you can create a sense of coherence and strengthen your themes and concepts.

Examples of Motifs in Popular Novels and Their Contribution to the Overall Theme

In "The Great Gatsby" by F. Scott Fitzgerald, the green light is a symbol that represents Gatsby's longing for lost love and the corrupting nature of wealth. In "The Sound and the Fury" by William Faulkner, the recurring motif of time highlights themes of decay and the fleeting nature of life, as well as the characters' struggles with memory and identity.

Avoiding Heavy-Handed Symbolism in Writing

To avoid overly obvious symbolism, an author can use more subtle symbols that require interpretation from the reader. For instance, instead of using a rose to symbolize love, the author could use a wilted flower to suggest a dying relationship. Also, an author should use symbols only when they are essential to the story, rather than overusing them. Keep in mind that the symbolism should complement and not distract from the story.

Tips for Creating Symbols with Multiple Layers of Meaning

To create symbols that have many different meanings, think about objects, actions, or events that have a personal connection to you. These symbols are more likely to connect with your readers and evoke different interpretations. Remember that the meaning of a symbol can change depending on the situation in which it is used. For example, a snake can be seen as dangerous or evil, but it can also represent wisdom or transformation depending on the context.

Using Motifs to Connect Different Parts of a Story and Create Cohesion

Motifs can be used to link various parts of a story and create a unified and cohesive narrative. This can be done by using repeating images, like a particular color or object, that is associated with a character, place, or theme. Alternatively, repeating themes or ideas can be used, which are further explored and developed throughout the story. Consistent use of motifs can strengthen the themes and ideas of the story, bringing everything together in a seamless and meaningful way.

<h1 style="text-align:center">51</h1>

Experiment with non-linear storytelling techniques to keep readers engaged

Using non-linear storytelling can make your story more interesting by adding layers of complexity and depth. It can also create a sense of mystery and intrigue by presenting events out of order. By exploring the different perspectives and experiences of your characters, you can create a more complex story. However, non-linear storytelling can be more challenging for readers to follow than traditional linear narratives, use it carefully. When done well, non-linear storytelling can be a powerful tool for creating a memorable and engaging story.

Examples of non-linear storytelling in popular fiction and their impact on the reader's experience

A popular example of non-linear storytelling is "The Time Traveler's Wife" by Audrey Niffenegger. The story follows the love story of a man with a genetic disorder that causes him to time travel involuntarily and his wife who must cope with his sporadic absences. The story jumps back and forth between different points in time, creating a sense of mystery and a deeper understanding of the characters' experiences. Another example is "Cloud Atlas" by David Mitchell, which consists of six interconnected stories set in different time periods, woven together to create a larger, more complex narrative. This technique shows how events in one time period can impact events in another, creating a sense of unity and connection throughout the story.

Effectively using non-linear storytelling techniques without confusing the reader

To use non-linear storytelling effectively, authors should give readers clear markers that help them keep track of the story. For instance, they could label chapters with information about the time and place of events, or use different fonts and formatting to indicate different perspectives. Moreover, have a clear narrative thread that runs through the story, even if the events don't occur in chronological order. This could involve using recurring themes or symbols or establishing a central goal or conflict that drives the plot forward. Above all, authors should trust that their readers are intelligent enough to follow a non-linear narrative, even if it requires some effort to piece together.

Using non-linear storytelling to create mystery and suspense in your story

Using non-linear storytelling can be an effective way to create a sense of intrigue and suspense in a story. By revealing information in a non-chronological order or withholding details, you can make readers curious and uncertain. For instance, you could use flashbacks to gradually reveal important details about a character's past, building up to a significant reveal that changes how the reader perceives the story. Alternatively, you could use a non-linear structure to hint at future events or revelations, creating a sense of anticipation without giving away too much information.

52

Consider how the setting and world-building affect the plot

To make a story more engaging, create a detailed and immersive setting. This can be achieved by using descriptive language that appeals to the reader's senses, and considering how the environment impacts the characters and story. A well-crafted setting can also help to establish the tone and themes of the story, allowing the reader to fully immerse themselves in the fictional world and become invested in the characters and plot.

Examples of Novels where Setting and World-Building Impact the Story

"The Hunger Games" by Suzanne Collins and "The Lord of the Rings" trilogy by J.R.R. Tolkien are two examples of novels where the setting and world-building are important parts of the story. In "The Hunger Games," the dystopian setting and futuristic technology add to the tension and contribute to the theme of rebellion. In "The Lord of the Rings," the vast and varied landscape of Middle-earth and its different races and cultures contribute to the themes of friendship, courage, and the fight against evil.

Balancing Detailed World-Building with Plot Progression

Balance the amount of world-building in their story. They should introduce elements of their world slowly to avoid overwhelming readers with too much information at once. Also, authors should make sure that their world-building is relevant to the plot and characters, and avoid including any unnecessary details.

Common Mistakes in Setting and World-Building and How to Avoid Them

One mistake that authors often make is giving too much information about the world in a way that feels unnatural. Another mistake is not considering how the world they create impacts the story and the characters. To avoid these mistakes, authors should focus on creating a world that feels real and natural, rather than just providing a long list of details.

Conveying Themes and Messages through Setting and World-Building

The environment and world-building can be utilized by authors to express important themes and messages in various ways. The setting can mirror the characters' inner turmoil or symbolize significant social problems. The world-building can also help examine themes such as power, identity, and culture, as well as create an atmosphere that fits the story's themes. Through setting and world-building, writers can reinforce the story's messages and themes, leading to a more profound and meaningful reading experience.

53

Use subplots to add complexity and depth to your story

Including subplots in a story can enhance its depth and complexity. Subplots can contribute to character development, world-building, and theme exploration. They also help to maintain reader engagement.

Example of a Well-Executed Subplot in a Popular Novel

The Harry Potter series by J.K. Rowling is a great example of a story with multiple subplots. For instance, the ongoing conflict between the Order of the Phoenix and the Death Eaters adds more excitement and complexity to the plot, while also providing readers with a better insight into the world and the characters.

Balancing the Main Plot with Subplots

The main plot of a story should always be the focus, but subplots can also be important. To balance the two, an author should ensure that each subplot relates to the main plot and contributes to the overall themes of the story. Subplots should also not distract too much from the main plot or overwhelm the reader.

Understanding the difference between subplots and distractions in your story

A subplot is like a smaller storyline within a larger story, which connects to and enriches the main plot. Subplots can make the story more interesting and help in developing the characters. However, distractions are elements that don't contribute to the story or characters and can pull the reader's attention away from the intended focus. Distractions can be things like unnecessary details, characters, or events that don't add to the overall story or characters.

Ensuring subplots enhance, not distract from the main plot of your story

If you want your subplots to enhance your main plot, make sure they connect to the main story in a significant way. You can do this by making sure the subplot relates to the main character's journey, or by providing additional context or backstory that makes the main story more interesting. To avoid distractions, limit the number of subplots you include and make sure they are well-developed with clear arcs and resolutions that tie into the main plot.

Using Subplots to Develop Secondary Characters

Subplots can help to develop supporting characters and add more depth to their personalities. By providing them with their own storylines, an author can explore their motivations, desires, and fears, creating a more well-rounded and relatable character. This also helps to make the story world more engaging, providing the reader with a better understanding of the characters and the world they exist in.

The negative impact of too many subplots on the main plot of your story

Stay focused on the main plot of your story. Adding too many subplots or distractions can water down the effect of your main plot and make it harder for readers to follow and get emotionally invested in the story. Furthermore, subplots and distractions can divert attention from the development of your primary characters and their journeys, thereby reducing the impact of your story's resolution.

Determining essential subplots in your story and eliminating unnecessary ones

To decide which subplots are important, ask yourself if they add value to the main plot or characters. If a subplot doesn't contribute anything significant to the story's resolution or the character's development, it's likely a distraction that can be removed. You can also create a summary of your main plot and characters, and analyze the subplots to see how they fit in.

Examples of novels with a strong and focused plot

There are some fantastic examples of novels that have a strong and focused plot. For instance, we have "To Kill a Mockingbird" by Harper Lee, "1984" by George Orwell, and "The Great Gatsby" by F. Scott Fitzgerald. These books have captivating and straightforward main plots, with well-crafted characters and minimal distractions or subplots that take away from the main storyline.

Reasons for Including Unnecessary Scenes or Subplots in a Story

Writers may include unnecessary scenes or subplots in their stories due to personal attachment or external pressure to meet certain expectations. However, keep in mind that every element in the story should contribute to the overall narrative.

Balancing the Main Plot, Character Development, and World-Building in a Story

An effective technique is to ensure that each scene and subplot contributes to multiple aspects of the story. For instance, a scene that moves the plot forward can also provide insight into a character or the story's world. Additionally, building character and world-building around the main plot can create a more coherent and impactful story. This approach centers on exploring how the main plot impacts the characters and the world, leading to a more integrated and compelling narrative.

54

Use the three-act structure to help organize your story into a beginning, middle, and end.

The three-act structure is a popular way of telling stories in books, movies, and plays. It breaks down the story into three parts: the beginning where the setting, characters, and the main problem are introduced; the middle where the problem becomes more difficult, and the characters face challenges; and the end where the problem is solved, and everything comes together nicely.

By using this structure, you can create a compelling story that keeps your readers hooked and has a satisfying ending. It's a tried-and-true method that ensures your story has a strong foundation.

Deviating from the Three-Act Structure: How to Determine if it Enhances or Detracts from Your Story

Remember that while the three-act structure is helpful, it's not the only way to tell a story. It can be beneficial to deviate from the norm, but only if it helps your story. Before doing so, consider why you want to change the structure. Will it make the story better or more engaging, or will it confuse readers? Will it enhance the characters and themes, or take away from them? If the deviation is beneficial to the story and the reader, then it's worth considering.

Exploring Other Narrative Frameworks for Your Story Planning

There are various other ways to organize a story besides the three-act structure. Some examples include the hero's journey, the seven-point story structure, and the save the cat beat sheet. These frameworks have their unique advantages and disadvantages, so it's essential to select the one that fits your writing style and story.

Balancing Structure and Creativity: Effectively Using the Three-Act Structure

The main idea is to use the three-act structure as a tool to help tell the story, but not be restricted by it. Let the story develop naturally, while still following the basic structure. Adding surprising and original elements to each part can make the story more exciting. Create a story that captivates the reader, with well-crafted characters and a satisfying ending.

Can Deviating from Established Narrative Frameworks Make Your Story More Memorable?

When you deviate from the norm, you have the potential to create a story that is remarkable and unforgettable. However, make sure that you do it in a way that serves the purpose of the story and not just for the sake of being unconventional.

Striking the perfect balance between structure and creativity is crucial for an engaging and memorable story.

The Benefits of the Three-Act Structure for Organizing a Story

The three-act structure is a useful tool for authors as it provides a clear and organized framework to create a compelling story. It ensures that the story progresses smoothly, with a balanced pace and builds towards an exciting resolution. This technique helps writers to stay focused on the main conflict and ensure that every element of the story works towards the overall narrative.

Common Mistakes to Avoid when Using the Three-Act Structure in Writing

One mistake that writers make is sticking too closely to the three-act structure and not allowing the story to be flexible. Another mistake is not taking enough time to develop the story and characters, which can result in readers not being invested in the story. Additionally, some writers may give too much emphasis to the resolution and not enough attention to the confrontation, leading to a lack of excitement and tension.

Examples of Novels that Successfully Utilize the Three-Act Structure

Some novels that effectively use the three-act structure are "To Kill a Mockingbird" by Harper Lee, "The Hunger Games" by Suzanne Collins, and "The Great Gatsby" by F. Scott Fitzgerald. These books have a clear structure that builds tension and moves the story forward in a compelling way.

55

Avoid relying too heavily on coincidences or convenient plot developments.

To prevent unrealistic plot developments, it's essential to create characters that are believable and have distinct personalities. When your characters act in a way that's consistent with their motivations, it's easier to develop a story that feels genuine and unforced. Also, relying too much on coincidences should be avoided as it may lead to a contrived plot. Instead, writers should develop the story in a natural and logical way.

Common Pitfalls to Watch Out for When Developing a Plot

One mistake writers often make is relying too much on cliches or overused story elements. While it's okay to use these familiar elements, using them too much can make the story feel unoriginal and predictable. Strike a balance between familiar elements and fresh, unexpected twists that keep readers engaged. Another pitfall is trying to force the plot in a certain direction, which can lead to contrived or unrealistic developments. Instead, it's better to let the story evolve naturally based on the characters and their motivations.

Creating a Believable and Compelling Story without Relying on Coincidences

To make your story believable and interesting, you can concentrate on developing your characters and their motivations. It's essential to make sure their actions and decisions match their personalities and experiences. Additionally, you can create a well-organized plot with clear cause-and-effect relationships to make the story feel logical and credible. However, if you need to use coincidences or chance events, make sure they are justified and don't feel too artificial.

Using Foreshadowing to Create a Sense of Inevitability Without Relying on Coincidence

To make your story more exciting, you can use foreshadowing to hint at upcoming events. This technique can create a sense of suspense and excitement, keeping your readers engaged. To use foreshadowing effectively, you need to plan ahead and drop hints throughout the story that won't be noticed until later on. These clues should be subtle yet meaningful so that they make sense when looked back on. This way, you can create a feeling of inevitability without using coincidences or forced plot developments.

56

Create a compelling opening that hooks readers from the start

The beginning of your story sets the mood and lets readers know what to expect. It's your opportunity to get readers interested and eager to keep reading. If your story's start isn't engaging, readers might not want to continue reading. A captivating beginning gets readers hooked.

Effective Ways to Grab the Reader's Attention from the First Sentence

Starting your story with a bang grabs your reader's attention. You can achieve this by opening with a scene full of action or tension, introducing a character with a unique voice or backstory, or posing a question or bold statement that piques the reader's interest. The idea is to create a sense of curiosity and captivate the reader from the very beginning.

Setting the Tone and Establishing Themes in the Opening Pages

The first few pages of your story are a chance to give

the reader a taste of what's to come. You can do this by painting a picture with your words and setting the mood. If your story is sad or serious, you might describe something somber, like a Grey sky or a quiet room. If your story is about adventure or excitement, you might describe a thrilling scene. Be thoughtful and purposeful with your words so that your readers can get a sense of what your story is about.

Common Mistakes to Avoid in Your Story's Opening

When writing your story's opening, there are some common mistakes that you should avoid. One of these is starting with a lot of explanation or backstory all at once, which can be overwhelming for readers. Another mistake is starting with a cliche or overused idea, such as a character waking up to an alarm clock. Lastly, balance action with character development so that readers can connect with your story's protagonist.

57

Avoid excessive exposition or backstory in the early chapters

Providing background information, known as exposition, is crucial to a story, but avoid overloading the early chapters with too much exposition. Too much exposition can make the story feel slow and uninteresting, so balance the information and keep the readers engaged.

Effective ways to incorporate necessary backstory without overwhelming the reader

Incorporate the necessary backstory into the story in a way that feels organic and natural. This can be achieved by revealing information through dialogue or action, which keeps the story moving forward and engages readers. The goal is to integrate backstory seamlessly into the plot, rather than presenting it as a clunky and boring info dump.

Examples of novels that handle exposition well

Two excellent examples of novels that handle exposition well are "To Kill a Mockingbird" by Harper Lee and "The Great

Gatsby" by F. Scott Fitzgerald. In "To Kill a Mockingbird," Lee quickly moves into the action of the story while gradually revealing more about the characters and their pasts through dialogue and action. In "The Great Gatsby," Fitzgerald introduces the reader to the character of Gatsby through the eyes of the narrator, Nick Carraway, allowing the reader to gradually learn about Gatsby's past as the story unfolds.

Common mistakes authors make with exposition in the early chapters

Some authors make the mistake of beginning their story with a long and detailed explanation of the backstory, which can bore the reader and slow down the pace of the story. Another mistake is to give too much information all at once, which can confuse and overwhelm the reader. Finally, some authors focus too much on the backstory, neglecting the importance of the present action of the story, leading to a story that lacks excitement and engagement.

Determining the appropriate amount of exposition for a story

The amount of exposition needed varies according to the story. Weigh the impact of the information on the reader's understanding of the characters and the story's world, and incorporate it into the narrative in a way that seems logical and genuine. As a guideline, it's usually preferable to provide less exposition and allow the story to speak for itself.

IV

Writing Style And Techniques

58

Use sensory language to immerse readers in your world

One effective method for creating more captivating writing is to use sensory language. This means describing details that appeal to the reader's senses, such as sight, smell, taste, touch, and sound. By doing so, you can bring your story to life and make it more engaging for the reader.

To use sensory details in a natural way, it's best to be selective and use them purposefully. Instead of describing every sensory detail, pick out a few that will contribute to the mood and feeling of your writing. You can also incorporate sensory details in a way that flows seamlessly with your writing, instead of adding them as an afterthought. For instance, if your character is in a garden, you can describe how the scent of flowers surrounds them while they walk, instead of plainly saying that the garden smells good.

Which Senses to Focus on When Describing a Scene or Setting

When using sensory language, keep in mind that each scene or setting will require unique sensory descriptions. For instance, when describing a serene meadow, it's better to emphasize the vibrant colors of the flowers and the buzzing sound of the bees, while describing a gloomy alley would require the focus to be on the unpleasant odor of garbage and the feeling of discomfort.

Examples of How Sensory Language Enhances Writing

There are many sensory details you can use in your writing to create a vivid setting. You can describe the colors of objects, the sounds of the environment, the feel of the ground, the taste of food or drink, and the smells in the air. For instance, you can describe the sound of birds chirping in the morning, the feel of the cool grass under your feet, the smell of fresh bread baking in the oven, or the taste of salty ocean spray on your lips.

Here's an example that demonstrates the use of sensory language in writing:

"As Jane stepped into the bustling marketplace, the aroma of fresh spices and sizzling meats overwhelmed her senses. The colorful fabrics of the vendors' stalls caught her eye, and the lively chatter of merchants and customers alike filled her ears. She felt the rough texture of the cobblestone beneath her feet, and the heat of the midday sun beating down on her skin."

This example uses sensory language to vividly describe the setting of a busy marketplace, allowing the reader to imagine themselves in the scene and experience it through their senses

Balancing Sensory Language with Not Overloading the Reader

Use sensory language thoughtfully and do not flood the

reader with an excessive amount of detail. You want to provide enough sensory information to create a clear and vivid image in the reader's mind, but not so much that it becomes boring or overwhelming.

To strike a balance, focus on the most essential sensory details that contribute to the overall mood or tone of the scene. Additionally, vary the sensory descriptions throughout your writing, utilizing different senses to highlight various elements of the setting

Importance of Sensory Language in Creating a Strong Sense of Place in a Story

Using sensory language makes your readers feel like they are truly part of the story's world. By involving their senses, you can make the story more memorable and emotionally engaging. Sensory language also helps to set the tone of a scene and reveal character traits and emotions. However, Use sensory language appropriately, keeping in mind the reader's experience, and always use it strategically.

When you use descriptive language and sensory details in your writing, it can help readers imagine and feel what your characters are experiencing. This creates a deeper connection between the reader and the story, making it more powerful and memorable.

Common Mistakes to Avoid When Using Sensory Details in Writing

One mistake writers make is using too many sensory details, which can confuse the reader. Another mistake is relying on cliches, like comparing someone's eyes to diamonds. Finally, some writers don't connect their sensory details to the story, which makes them seem pointless. Use sensory details in a way that makes the story better and more engaging for the reader.

Using Sensory Details to Create Empathy with Characters

By using sensory details, writers can help readers empathize with characters by allowing them to experience the same sensations as the characters. This can create a strong emotional connection between the reader and the character. For example, if you describe a character feeling cold and wet in the rain, readers may understand and relate to their discomfort. Similarly, if you describe a character's pleasure in tasting a delicious meal, readers may feel happy along with the character. Overall, using sensory details can make the story more engaging and create a sense of shared experience between the reader and the character.

59

Show, don't tell – use descriptive language and sensory details to immerse readers in the story.

"Show, don't tell" is a writing technique that advises writers to use vivid descriptions and sensory details to engage readers in the story, instead of just telling them what's happening or how the characters are feeling. For instance, instead of saying "he was angry," a writer can describe the character's physical reactions like clenching fists, gritting teeth, or raising their voice to convey the emotion.

Immersing Readers with Descriptive Language and Sensory Details: Tips for Effective Writing

One way to make your writing more engaging is to use descriptive language and sensory details that appeal to the reader's five senses - sight, sound, smell, taste, and touch. By doing this, you can create a vivid and immersive experience that draws the reader into the story. Strong verbs and colorful adjectives can also help to bring your writing to life.

Common Mistakes to Avoid When Describing Scenes or Characters in Writing

One thing writers often do wrong is use too many adjectives or phrases that have become boring and overused, which can make their writing seem fake or exaggerated. Another mistake is writing passively or using generic phrases like "he felt sad" instead of showing how the character feels.

Examples of How Descriptive Language and Sensory Details Enhance Writing

Here's an example: Before: The house was old and dusty. After: As she stepped into the old house, the musty smell of dust and age hit her nose. The faded wallpaper peeled away from the walls, and the creaky floorboards groaned under her weight. The sunlight filtered in through the dirty windows, casting long, eerie shadows across the room. By using descriptive language and sensory details, we've created a more detailed and engaging scene that helps the reader imagine the old and dusty house.

Practicing "Show, Don't Tell": Tips for Writers to Improve Their Writing

One way to get better at "show, don't tell" is to rewrite a scene using descriptive language and sensory details instead of just telling what's happening. Reading books by other authors and observing how they use descriptive language and sensory details can also be helpful.

60

Vary your sentence structure and length to create rhythm and pacing

Changing the length and structure of sentences is crucial because it can make your writing more captivating. If your writing only has sentences that are the same length and structure, it can become dull and uninteresting. By varying the length and structure of your sentences, you can make your writing more exciting and maintain the reader's interest.

Tips for Varying Sentence Structure in Writing

To make your writing more interesting, you can change the way you write sentences. One way to do this is by using different sentence lengths, and types (like simple, compound, and complex), and starting and ending sentences differently.

The Impact of Sentence Structure on Pace and Tone

The way you structure your sentences can affect how fast or slow your writing feels and the overall mood of your piece. Short and simple sentences can make your writing feel fast-paced and tense, while longer and more complex sentences can slow things down and allow readers to contemplate what's happening. Changing your sentence structure can make your writing more interesting and engaging for readers.

Examples of How Varying Sentence Length and Structure Can Improve Writing

First version - "John walked to the store. He bought some milk. He walked back home. He poured himself a glass." This version is dull and has no rhythm.

Improved version - "John walked to the store with the sun beating down on his back. He found the dairy section and grabbed a carton of milk. Walking home, he was thankful for the warm summer day. Finally, he arrived home, poured himself a cold glass of milk and sat down to rest." By mixing short and long sentences and varying sentence structure, this new version becomes more engaging and interesting to read.

Common Mistakes in Sentence Structure

Using the same sentence structure repeatedly can make your writing seem boring. Also, using overly complicated sentence structures that might confuse the reader is another mistake. To avoid this, find a balance between simple and complex sentence structures, and use them in a way that achieves the desired effect.

Common Sentence Structures Used by Writers

There are different ways to structure a sentence, including simple sentences (with one main idea), compound sentences (with two or more main ideas joined by conjunction), complex sentences (with one main idea and one or more dependent ideas), dialogue, action sequences, descriptions, and internal thoughts. Varying the length and structure of these elements can add rhythm and flow to your writing and help control the pacing of your story.

Effective Techniques for Varying Sentence Length and Structure in Writing

To keep the writing interesting, writers can effectively vary sentence length and structure in a few ways. One way is to mix short and long sentences to create emphasis or provide more information. Another way is to use different types of sentences like questions or commands. This adds variety to the writing and makes it more dynamic.

Practice Tips for Varying Sentence Length and Structure in Writing

Practicing can help writers learn how to vary sentence length and structure. One way to practice is to write a paragraph or short story using only one sentence structure, like simple sentences. Then, writers can try rewriting the same paragraph or story using different types of sentences and lengths. Another way to practice is to read other writers' work and observe how they vary their sentence length and structure. This can give writers ideas and inspiration for their own writing.

61

Avoid unnecessary adverbs and adjectives

Adverbs and adjectives are words that describe or modify other words in a sentence, and they can be useful in providing more details or making your writing more colorful. However, using too many or using them when they're not needed can make your writing feel messy and distract you from the point you're trying to make. In short, necessary adverbs and adjectives are the ones that help clarify or add meaning to a sentence, while unnecessary ones are the ones that don't really contribute anything to the meaning and can be taken out without changing the sentence's overall message.

How to Identify Unnecessary Adverbs and Adjectives in Your Writing

You can identify if an adverb or adjective is unnecessary by reading the sentence out loud and asking if it contributes to the meaning or value of the sentence. If it doesn't, then it's likely unnecessary and can be removed. You can also check for words that are overused or cliched and replace them with more descriptive and specific language to make your writing more interesting.

Reasons Why Some Writers Overuse Adverbs and Adjectives

Sometimes, writers use too many adverbs and adjectives because they believe it will add more interest to their writing. However, this can make the writing hard to understand and confusing.

Adverbs and adjectives can help to describe and add detail to writing. However, when used excessively, they can weaken the writing. This is because they can make the writing feel cluttered, slow down the pace, and create a sense of distance between the reader and the story. Additionally, using too many modifiers can be a sign of lazy writing, which can make the writing feel flat and uninteresting.

Examples of Improving Sentences by Removing Unnecessary Adverbs and Adjectives

Let me give you an example.

Before: "Sarah walked slowly and carefully across the slippery, wet pavement." After: "Sarah walked across the wet pavement."

In this example, the sentence has three unnecessary words - "slowly," "carefully," and "slippery." By removing these words, the sentence becomes shorter and easier to read, while still conveying the same message.

Here's another example:

"The big, brown, furry bear slowly and quietly walked through the thick, green forest."

To make it better, we can replace some of the modifiers with stronger verbs and more specific nouns:

"The bear lumbered through the forest, its fur brushing against the leaves and branches."

By using the verb "lumbered" and describing the bear's actions and surroundings, we can paint a more vivid picture for the reader without relying on too many adverbs and adjectives.

Tips for Making Your Writing More Concise by Eliminating Unnecessary Adverbs and Adjectives

To make your writing more concise, you can remove words that aren't necessary or don't add meaning to your story. Another way is to use powerful and exact language that expresses the tone and meaning you want to convey, without relying on adverbs and adjectives. This will make your story more interesting and engaging for readers.

Alternatives to excessive use of adverbs and adjectives in writing

There are other methods to express meaning in writing without using too many adverbs and adjectives. You can use action words and precise nouns to create visual images and illustrate the story. Dialogue is also a great way to reveal characters personalities and emotions. Another option is to use figurative language, like metaphors and similes, to provide meaning and create striking depictions. These techniques can help readers connect with the story and make it more engaging.

For example, instead of writing "she walked quickly," you could write "she sprinted" or "she rushed." Another option is to use context and setting to imply the meaning, rather than explicitly stating it. For instance, instead of writing "the sky was dark and ominous," you could write "the storm clouds loomed overhead."

The impact of overusing adverbs and adjectives in writing

When writers use too many adverbs and adjectives, it can make the writing feel heavy and distant from the reader. The reader may lose interest and find the writing to be dull. It can also show that the writer is not putting in enough effort to choose the best words for the story, which can result in a lack of depth and excitement in the writing.

Appropriate use of adverbs and adjectives in writing

Adverbs and adjectives can have a purpose in writing, such as adding detail or creating a particular mood. Dialogue can also benefit from their use as they reveal character traits and emotions. Yet, avoid overusing them and use them only when necessary. It's better to use a few of them than too many.

62

Use active voice to create more engaging prose

Active voice is when the subject of a sentence does the action, while passive voice is when the subject receives the action. For example, "The cat chased the mouse" is active, while "The mouse was chased by the cat" is passive.

Why Active Voice is More Engaging Than Passive Voice

To create momentum in your writing, using an active voice is very important. When using active voice, the subject of the sentence performs the action, which creates a feeling of urgency and energy. It helps the reader feel like they are part of the story and experiencing it in real time. On the other hand, passive voice can slow down the pace of the writing and create a sense of disconnection between the reader and the story.

Example of How Active Voice Improves a Sentence

For example, let's say you have the sentence "The ball was caught by John." This is in passive voice and is not as interesting to read. By switching to active voice, you can say

"John caught the ball." This is more direct and engaging, making the reader feel like they are part of the action.

When to Use Passive Voice in Writing

Passive voice is suitable when the subject is not significant, unknown, or when the action itself is more important than the subject. For example, "The first book on mathematics was printed in the 15th century" emphasizes the importance of the event rather than the person who printed it.

Common Mistakes in Using Passive Voice

One mistake writers often make is using the verb "to be" followed by a past participle, like "was eaten by." This creates a passive sentence structure where the subject is being acted upon. Another mistake is using overly complicated sentences that make it hard to identify the subject and who is performing the action, which can cause confusion and make the writing unclear.

The Role of Strong Verbs in Creating Momentum

Powerful verbs are key to making your writing flow smoothly. They show exactly what is happening and carry more impact than weaker verbs. By using strong verbs, you can paint a clearer picture in your reader's minds and keep them engaged in your story. Moreover, they reduce the need for too many adverbs and adjectives, which can slow down your story. Choosing the right verbs creates an energetic and dynamic pace for your writing.

For example, instead of saying "She walked slowly," you could say "She trudged." The second sentence uses a stronger verb that creates a more detailed image for the reader.

Examples of How Active Voice and Strong Verbs Improve Writing

Here's an example of a sentence that lacks momentum: "The cat was chased by the dog and ran quickly away." Now, let's try to make it more engaging by using active voice and strong verbs: "The dog chased the cat, who darted away with lightning speed." By using active voice and strong verbs, we're able to create a more lively and captivating image for the reader. The sentence is now shorter and more exciting, which helps to keep the story moving forward

Practicing Active Voice and Strong Verbs in Writing

To get better at using active voice and strong verbs, you can start by looking at your writing and finding areas where you can make the action more immediate and specific. You can also read other authors to see how they use these techniques to create momentum in their writing. Writing exercises that focus on using active voice and strong verbs can also help.

If you want to use active voice more often, try practicing by rewriting sentences in active voice. Make sure you're putting the focus on the subject performing the action and pay attention to your word choices and sentence structures. It takes practice, but you'll eventually get the hang of it and your writing will become more powerful and interesting.

63

Be concise and avoid unnecessary repetition

Being concise means keeping your writing clear and to the point. It helps your readers to understand your ideas without getting lost in long and unnecessary details. It also shows that you respect your readers' time and attention, as they don't want to spend their time reading through unnecessary words and repetition.

Identifying and Eliminating Unnecessary Repetition in Writing

To find repetition in your writing, read it over and highlight any repeated words or phrases. Once you've found the repetition, try to reword your sentences or paragraphs to say the same thing without repeating yourself. You can do this by using different words that mean the same thing, changing the sentence structure, or using pronouns instead of repeating nouns.

Examples of Distracting Repetition in Writing

Imagine you're telling a story and you describe someone's hair as "blond" multiple times in a single paragraph. This repetition can make the story seem boring and uninteresting. Instead, you can use other words or rephrase the descriptions to make the story more captivating and fun to read.

Common Culprits of Unnecessary Repetition in Writing

A few things that can lead to repetition in writing are using the same words or phrases over and over again, adding extra descriptive words that don't add value, and repeating information that has already been stated. To avoid repetition, you should try to be mindful of these habits and work to eliminate them from your writing.

Making Your Writing More Concise without Sacrificing Clarity or Meaning

To make your writing shorter and clearer, remove any words or phrases that don't add meaning to the sentence. Use active voice and strong verbs to convey your message in fewer words. Avoid repeating the same information too much, as it can be boring. By doing these things, you can make your writing more concise without making it harder to understand.

64

Avoid using cliches or overused phrases.

Cliches are common phrases or sayings that have been used so much they have become unoriginal and uninspiring. They make writing seem dull and lacking in imagination. Readers may think the writer has not put enough thought into their work if they come across cliches. So, writers should stay away from cliches to keep their writing engaging, fresh, and creative.

Tips for Creating Original and Unique Phrases in Writing

To avoid using overused phrases, writers should think outside of the box and come up with new and exciting ways to express their ideas. This means being specific and creative with their language. Using metaphors, similes, and descriptive language can help to make writing more unique and engaging. Think about the context of the story and the characters involved, as this can inspire original phrases and expressions that fit the setting and tone of the piece.

Common Cliches and Overused Phrases Writers Should Avoid

Writers should steer clear of using common phrases that have been used so many times that they have lost their original meaning and impact. Examples of such phrases include "all is fair in love and war," "time heals all wounds," "in the nick of time," "every cloud has a silver lining," and "the calm before the storm." Readers are likely to find them unoriginal and boring.

The Negative Impact of Using Cliches and Overused Phrases in Writing

Using cliches or overused phrases can make writing feel boring and lacking in creativity. It can also make the writing seem like it was done without much effort. When readers come across cliches, they might think that the writer didn't try hard enough to come up with something original. This can cause readers to lose interest in the story and the characters, which can make the reading experience less enjoyable.

Improving Your Writing by Avoiding Cliches and Overused Phrases: Examples and Techniques

Instead of using a cliche like "the calm before the storm," you can paint a more vivid picture by using specific and descriptive language. For example, "the air was still, the leaves on the trees motionless, and the sky an eerie shade of green as if it were holding its breath before unleashing a fury of rain and wind." This not only avoids the cliche but also creates a more immersive and engaging image for the reader. Similarly, instead of using the cliche "time heals all wounds," you can show the character's emotional wounds still being present even after a long time has passed, adding depth and complexity to the character and their story.

65

Use literary devices like metaphor, symbolism and other figurative language to add depth to your writing

Figurative language is a type of language that uses words in a way that goes beyond their ordinary meaning to make a more interesting and imaginative impact. On the other hand, literal language is a plain and simple way of conveying information. Figurative language makes use of techniques such as comparisons, exaggeration, giving non-human things human-like characteristics, and more to create lively images and express abstract concepts.

Common Types of Figurative Language Used in Writing

Figurative language includes different techniques that writers use to make their writing more interesting and engaging. Some of these techniques are similes and metaphors, which compare two things to create a vivid image. Personification is when human characteristics are given to things that are not human. Hyperbole is used to exaggerate to create emphasis or effect. Symbolism is when objects or ideas represent something else.

Understanding Metaphors and Their Use in Writing

Metaphor is a tool used in writing to compare two things that may seem different but have similarities. It can help you to create more vivid descriptions and express complex ideas in a simpler way. For instance, saying "life is a stage" compares life to performance and adds more meaning to your writing.

How Metaphors and Similes Add Depth and Complexity to Writing

Metaphors and similes are like magic tricks that make writing more exciting and imaginative. They can help readers understand difficult concepts by showing them in a new and fascinating way. With metaphors and similes, writers can make their work more meaningful and encourage readers to think more deeply about what they're reading.

Common Metaphors and Similes Used in Writing

Metaphors and similes come in many forms, but the most effective ones are often tailored to the subject of the writing. A few examples of metaphors are "life is a journey" or "love is a rose", while similes might use "like" or "as" to compare things, like "her voice was like honey" or "the wind howled like a wolf".

Adding Meaning through Symbolism in Writing

Symbolism is when you use something specific to represent a larger, more complex idea or emotion. A symbol can be an object, an action, or an image. In "The Great Gatsby," the green light at the end of Daisy's dock is a symbol of Gatsby's longing for a future with her. This adds meaning and emotion to the story.

Balancing Literary Devices in Writing

To use literary devices in your writing, it's essential to make them blend in seamlessly with your story. Your devices should emerge effortlessly from your characters, setting, or plot and not appear contrived or artificial. Also, you should avoid overusing these devices and relying on them excessively. Instead, use them to enrich your writing subtly.

Common Mistakes When Using Literary Devices in Writing

A common error is to use too many literary devices, which can make the writing appear unnatural or forced. Another mistake is to use them in an obvious or clichéd way, which can feel cheesy. It's essential to use literary devices in a deliberate and meaningful way that complements the story.

Potential Drawbacks of Overusing Figurative Language in Your Writing

Using too much figurative language in a story can make it hard for readers to follow the plot and understand the message. It can also be confusing if the reader doesn't know the meaning of the language used. So, use it carefully and appropriately to create the desired impact on the reader.

Enhancing Writing with the Natural Use of Literary Devices

To incorporate literary devices in your writing, try to make them emerge naturally from your story's elements such as characters, settings, or themes. You can also learn from other authors by reading their works and analyzing how they use literary devices to enhance their writing. With practice and experimentation, you can strike a balance and use literary devices effectively in your own writing.

Effectively Using Figurative Language to Create Vivid Images in Writing

To effectively use figurative language, writers can try using comparisons that are not typical, so that readers can see things in a fresh and interesting way. It's also helpful to use descriptive language that appeals to the senses, making the reader feel like they are really there. Additionally, writers can use figurative language to set the mood or tone of the writing, choosing comparisons that elicit a specific emotion or atmosphere.

Examples of How Figurative Language Can Improve Writing

Figurative language can greatly improve your writing. For instance, instead of saying "the sun was shining brightly," you can use a metaphor like "the sun was a brilliant starburst in the sky." This provides a more descriptive and lasting image in the reader's mind. Alternatively, you can use personification to give objects human-like characteristics, such as "the wind whispered secrets through the trees." This helps to create a particular mood and tone in the scene.

Practicing Using Figurative Language in Writing

To improve using figurative language in your writing, you can read works of authors who use it well and study their techniques. Additionally, you can try writing exercises that challenge you to come up with unique and creative comparisons. Practicing regularly is important for developing your skills and incorporating figurative language into your writing style.

To create a unique writing style using figurative language, you can try different types and combinations of techniques that speak to you. However, always remember that the purpose of using figurative language is to enrich the story and engage the reader, so maintain clarity and coherence while experimenting with style.

66

Read widely and study the writing of authors you admire

As a writer, read many different types of books and written works. Doing so allows you to experience a variety of writing styles, viewpoints, and ideas. By expanding your reading horizons, you'll develop a better understanding of the world and gain inspiration for your own writing.

How Studying Other Authors' Writing Can Improve Your Own Writing

Reading the works of other writers can help you improve your writing skills. You can learn a lot from observing their writing techniques, such as how they use dialogue, characterization, plot, and pacing. You can also learn how they use language and literary devices to create different effects or moods. This can inspire you to try new things and improve your own writing.

Analyzing the Writing of an Author You Admire: What to Look For

When studying the work of an author you admire, focus on specific techniques and elements that make their writing exceptional. Look at their use of language, dialogue, description, and other literary devices. Consider how they structure their sentences and paragraphs, and how they use pacing and tension to create a sense of excitement or suspense. Also, think about how they create interesting characters and build a strong sense of place.

Balancing Reading for Pleasure and Reading to Improve Your Writing

As a writer, find a balance between reading for pleasure and reading to enhance your skills. While exploring different genres and authors can teach you valuable writing techniques, take a break and enjoy reading purely for fun. This can help you relax, recharge your creativity, and gain inspiration for your own work. However, when you do read to improve your writing, be intentional and focused on what you want to learn from the material.

The Benefits of Reading Outside Your Preferred Genre or Style

Venturing beyond your favorite genre or writing style can be a great way to enhance your writing skills. It allows you to discover new concepts, themes, and techniques that you may have never encountered before. Reading a diverse range of literature can also expand your horizon and give you a fresh perspective. Moreover, it can help you break free from common cliches or overused tropes that often plague a particular genre or style.

67

Experiment with different perspectives, including first-person, third-person limited, and third-person omniscient

First-person perspective is when the story is told from the point of view of a character using words like "I" or "we." It can make readers feel close to the narrator, but they might miss out on other events and characters in the story. Third-person perspective is told from an objective point of view using "he," "she," or "they." Third-person limited means the story is told from one character's point of view, while third-person omniscient means the narrator can access the thoughts and feelings of all the characters.

The Impact of Perspective on the Reader's Perception of a Story

When you change the perspective of a story, it can change the reader's perception and experience of it. For instance, first-person perspective can create a feeling of urgency and immediacy, while third-person limited can give the reader insight into multiple characters' perspectives while still maintaining a close connection to one character's thoughts and feelings. A third-person omniscient perspective can provide an objective view of the story's events, giving the reader a bigger picture.

Benefits of Writing in First-Person Perspective

Writing in the first-person perspective can make the story more personal and emotional. It can help readers connect with the narrator and understand their thoughts and feelings in a more profound way. Furthermore, it can allow the author to delve into the narrator's psyche, shedding light on their behavior and decisions.

Benefits of Writing in Third-Person Limited or Omniscient Perspective

In the third-person limited perspective, an author can delve deeper into the thoughts and emotions of one character while keeping a level of impartiality. On the other hand, the third-person omniscient perspective can help an author provide a comprehensive view of the story's events and characters by accessing their thoughts and feelings.

Choosing the Right Perspective for Your Story or Scene

Choosing the perspective to tell a story depends on the desired effect and the story itself. First-person perspective can be useful for creating a strong bond between the reader and narrator, while third-person limited or omniscient perspective can provide an objective view of events. When deciding on the best perspective to use, consider the tone, themes, and characters of the story.

68

Show character emotions through actions and dialogue, rather than telling the reader how they feel

Show character emotions in your story because it makes it more interesting and draws the reader in. When the reader can feel the emotions of the character through their actions and words, they become more involved and invested in the story. This makes it more memorable and can leave a lasting impression on the reader.

Common mistakes when showing character emotions

Writers sometimes make the mistake of using too many internal thoughts or long monologues to show emotions, instead of expressing them through character actions and words. Another mistake is using too many adjectives and adverbs to describe emotions, instead of letting the reader experience them through the character's behavior. Finally, some writers may try too hard to be obvious in their portrayal of emotions, which can seem forced or fake.

Using dialogue to convey emotions effectively

Using dialogue to convey emotions effectively can be a great way to bring your characters to life, but avoid being too direct or obvious. Instead, use subtle cues like tone of voice or choice of words to give readers a sense of what the character is feeling. For example, a character who is feeling sad might say "I'm okay," but in a way that lets the reader know they're not really okay. This kind of dialogue can create a more authentic and relatable portrayal of your characters.

Nonverbal cues for indicating character emotions

Nonverbal cues are actions or behaviors that can indicate a character's emotional state, such as facial expressions, body language, and gestures. For instance, a character who feels nervous might fidget with their hands or avoid eye contact, while an angry character might clench their fists or grit their teeth. These details can add realism to your characters and help the reader understand and connect with their emotions.

Using character emotions to drive the plot

Character emotions can be a significant force that moves your story forward. By giving your characters intense and unique emotions, you can generate drama and suspense that propel the plot. For instance, a character's fear or longing could drive them to take action, while their envy or fury could lead them to make choices that have unforeseen outcomes. By using character emotions to create momentum and urgency, you can keep your readers hooked and interested in the narrative.

69

Use humor to lighten the tone of your writing, but be careful not to overdo it

Using humor in writing can have a great impact on the reader as it makes the writing more interesting and the characters more memorable. It can also be used to add some lightness to serious situations. It can make your writing more appealing and easier for the audience to connect with.

Examples of Successful Use of Humor in Literature

Many well-known books have effectively used humor to create engaging stories, like the clever and funny conversations between Elizabeth Bennet and Mr Darcy in "Pride and Prejudice" by Jane Austen, the imaginative and silly scenarios in "Alice's Adventures in Wonderland" by Lewis Carroll, and the witty commentary on society in "The Adventures of Huckleberry Finn" by Mark Twain.

Balancing Humor with Serious Themes in Writing

Balancing humor and serious themes in writing requires skillful handling, as humor should not undermine the seriousness of a situation. One way to balance them is to use it as a way to provide relief during tense moments while still preserving the emotional impact. Another way is to use it to highlight the irony or absurdity of a serious situation, which can engage the reader more deeply with the theme.

Using Humor to Create Memorable Characters

Using humor can help make characters more memorable and likable to readers. One way to achieve this is by giving characters a distinct and relatable sense of humor that reflects their personality and worldview. Additionally, using it can reveal a character's vulnerabilities, quirks, and imperfections, making them more relatable and human to readers.

Determining When Humor is Appropriate in Writing

The decision to use humor in your writing depends on various factors, including the style, genre, and intended readers of your work. In general, it should be used in a way that matches the tone and theme of your writing and does not take away from the seriousness of important moments. It's also crucial to consider cultural differences and avoid it that may be inappropriate or hurtful.

70

Use research to add authenticity and credibility to your writing

Research plays a vital role in writing since it makes your work more convincing and trustworthy. It enhances the credibility and appeal of your story to the reader. Accurate details about a topic make your characters and settings more lively and authentic.

Common Research Methods for Writers

Writers use various methods to conduct research, depending on their type of writing. Some common methods include reading, interviewing experts, attending events, visiting relevant places, and conducting online research.

Adding Depth to Characters and Settings with Research

Research can assist you in comprehending the characters' motivations and experiences, as well as the historical, cultural, and social contexts of your narrative. By investigating the era, culture, or place where your story occurs, you can include precise details that will make your narrative more captivating and lifelike for your readers.

Using Research to Write About Unfamiliar Topics

When you're writing about a topic that you don't have much knowledge about, research is crucial. Through research, you can learn about the topic and gather accurate information that you can use to create a compelling story. Be open-minded and consider different perspectives when conducting your research.

Balancing Research with Creative Ideas in Writing

Finding the right balance between research and creativity can be tricky, but it's crucial for creating a captivating story. One way to do this is to conduct your research first and then use your imagination to blend it into your story. Alternatively, you can let your creative ideas lead your research, so you can concentrate on the parts that matter most to your story. Ultimately, the goal is to achieve a balance that showcases an engaging narrative while incorporating truthful and genuine information.

71

Create compelling, well-rounded settings that add to the story

Make your story's setting interesting because it can set the mood of the story, provide important information for the reader and make them feel like they're part of the story. A good setting can transport the reader to a different world and make them feel like they're really there.

Using setting to add depth to stories

An effective way to use setting is to make it an important part of the story. It should not just be a background but should be an active and dynamic component that affects the characters and events. Additionally, the way characters interact with their surroundings can reveal important information about their personality and motivations. Lastly, the setting can be used to create conflict and tension by placing characters in a challenging or unsettling environment.

Common mistakes when describing settings in writing

Providing too many details about the setting can be overwhelming and slow down the pace of the story. Leave room for the reader's imagination. Also, the setting should be integrated into the story in a way that feels connected and interesting. If the setting feels disconnected, it can make the story fall flat.

Ensuring settings are well-rounded and add to the story

To make sure that the setting of your story is well-rounded, it's a good idea to think of it like a character. Think about its history, personality, and motivations. Also, include unique details like sights, sounds, and smells that will make the setting come to life. Pay attention to how the setting changes over time. Lastly, make sure the setting plays a role in the story and is not just in the background.

Examples of stories effectively using setting to enhance the overall story

An example is the book "The Great Gatsby" by F. Scott Fitzgerald. The story takes place in the 1920s, a time of lavish parties and excess, which shapes the plot and characters' actions. The descriptions of the parties and characters' luxurious lifestyles help set the mood and tone.

Another example is "To Kill a Mockingbird" by Harper Lee. The story takes place in a small southern town during the 1930s, where racial tensions are high. The town's descriptions help establish context and reveal character motivations, showing how the setting plays an integral part in the story.

72

Use dialogue tags sparingly and make sure they're clear and unobtrusive.

Dialogue tags are phrases that let readers know which character is speaking in a conversation. They help readers follow the conversation and understand what is happening. Without dialogue tags, readers may become confused about who is saying what.

Writing Effective Dialogue Tags: Tips for Avoiding Distractions

Using dialogue tags effectively means using them in moderation and making sure they don't take away from the conversation itself. Instead of always using "he said" or "she said," authors can be more creative and use tags like "whispered," "muttered," or "exclaimed" to show the mood or emotion of the dialogue. Additionally, authors can use action beats to indicate who's speaking instead of just using dialogue tags, like having a character grin before saying, "I'm so happy."

Common Mistakes in Using Dialogue Tags and How to Avoid

Them

Using too many dialogue tags can be distracting and take away from the story. Overly complicated tags, like "he ejaculated" or "she interrogated", can sound forced or awkward. Additionally, it's best to avoid using adverbs to modify dialogue tags, like "he said loudly" or "she said softly" because they can weaken the impact of the dialogue.

Improving Writing with Clear and Unobtrusive Dialogue Tags: Examples

Here's an example to show how using clear and unobtrusive dialogue tags can improve a piece of writing:

In the first version of the scene, the dialogue tags were distracting and took away from the conversation. But in the second version, the tags were simpler and allowed the reader to focus on what the characters were saying. By using clear and concise tags, the dialogue flows naturally and the reader can follow along easily. Additionally, the characters' actions help to convey their emotions and intentions, creating a more immersive reading experience

Practicing Dialogue Tags: Tips for Using Them Sparingly and Effectively

To practice using dialogue tags effectively, you can read books by other writers and notice how they use tags and action beats. Another way is to write a scene without dialogue tags and add them later only when necessary. This can help writers understand when and where tags are needed. Lastly, reading the dialogue out loud can help writers ensure that it flows smoothly and make changes if necessary.

V

Editing And Revision

73

Take time away from your writing before revising

If you want to make your writing better, it's a good idea to take a break before you start making changes. Taking a break improves your work a lot.

How Long to Wait Before Revising Your Work

The duration of a break can differ for each writer depending on their individual requirements. A brief break, such as a few hours or a day, may be sufficient for some writers, while others may benefit from a longer break lasting a week or more. It's essential to pay attention to your body and take a break when you require it, rather than overworking yourself. This helps you to look at your writing with fresh eyes as if you were seeing it for the first time.

Benefits of Taking a Break Before Revising Writing

Taking a break from your writing can be incredibly beneficial for improving the quality of your revisions. It gives your brain a chance to rest and recover. Writing and editing can be tiring for the mind, and taking breaks can prevent you from becoming exhausted and enable you to approach your work with a renewed perspective. When you do this, you can spot any problems or mistakes you might have missed before. Also, taking a break can give you a chance to relax and clear your mind, improving a writer's mental and emotional well-being so you can focus better, leading to even more beautiful writing.

The Necessity of Taking Breaks Before Revising Writing

While it's not a requirement, it's strongly advised to take some time off from your writing before you start revising. However, if you're short on time and can't take a break, you can still revise your writing skillfully, but be mindful that you may overlook certain errors or shortcomings in your work.

Resisting the Urge to Immediately Revise Your Writing

It can be challenging to resist the temptation to revise your writing immediately, especially when you're excited about improving it. However, remember that revising too soon may have negative consequences. To avoid revising too early, try scheduling a specific time frame for taking a break from your work before revising. You can choose to take a few days, a week, or longer, depending on what suits you best. During this time, focus on other activities and give yourself a break from writing. When you return to your work, you'll feel more refreshed and ready to tackle revisions with a clear head.

Signs That a Writer Needs a Break

There are a few indicators that a writer may need to take a break, such as feeling stuck or frustrated with their writing, facing writer's block, or experiencing mental exhaustion. If you're finding it hard to concentrate on your work or not making much headway, it's probably a good idea to take a break.

Activities to Recharge Creativity During a Writer's Break

Writers can do many activities during their break to replenish their creativity, such as going for a walk, practicing meditation or yoga, reading a book, spending time with loved ones, or engaging in a hobby. Choose an activity that brings joy and helps to unwind and recharge.

74

Keep the audience in mind when making editing decisions

When editing your work, keep in mind who will be reading it – your audience. By understanding your audience, you can make smart choices about what to include in your writing, what to leave out, and how to present it to them. Writing that is designed for your audience is more likely to be engaging and successful, while writing that ignores your audience's interests or needs may not connect with them.

Determining Your Target Audience as a Writer

To successfully reach your readers, determine your target audience – the individuals who are most likely to be captivated by your writing. Begin by reflecting on the genre and subject matter of your writing, as well as your writing style and tone. Delve into the minds of potential readers and consider their demographic characteristics, including age, gender, educational background, and cultural heritage. Additionally, seeking input from beta readers or conducting market research can provide valuable insights into your target audience.

Tailoring Your Writing to Your Intended Audience

When editing your work, keep your intended audience in mind and make decisions that cater to their needs and expectations. This involves using language that is suitable for their reading level, providing relevant context or background information, and using a tone that resonates with their preferences. Additionally, you can think about the format and presentation of your writing, including the incorporation of visual or interactive elements to enhance engagement.

Avoiding Confusion or Alienation of Your Audience

To ensure that your audience understands and engages with your writing, communicate your ideas clearly and concisely. Avoid using technical language or jargon that your readers may not be familiar with, and provide enough context to help them follow your train of thought. Seeking feedback from beta readers or conducting user testing can also help you identify areas that may cause confusion or need improvement in your writing.

Using Beta Reader Feedback to Understand Your Audience and Their Needs

Feedback from beta readers can be very helpful in understanding your readers and what they need. You should pay close attention to the feedback you receive and try to find any patterns or themes that come up. This can help you see which parts of your writing are most interesting or confusing for your readers, and where you might need to make some changes to meet their needs better. You can also ask your beta readers some questions about their reading experience, such as whether they found your writing easy to read and interesting, or if they felt like your writing was meant for them.

<h1 style="text-align:center">75</h1>

Use critique groups or beta readers to get feedback on your work

A critique group is a small team of writers who gather to give and receive feedback on their writing. You can locate them through local writing associations or online communities.

A beta reader is like a test reader who reads your book before it's published and offers feedback on specific areas like the plot, character growth, pacing, and writing style. You can find beta readers through social media, writing forums, or by asking your friends or relatives to read your writing.

Importance of Beta Readers for Providing Valuable Feedback

Beta readers can be super helpful because they can give you an outsider's opinion on your work and can find problems you might not have noticed. They can also tell you what readers might think of your story and help you figure out where you can make your writing better.

Beta readers can give you useful feedback in many ways. First, they can provide a different viewpoint on your writing. We writers tend to be too close to our own work to spot its problems and faults. They can help you discover any problems with the story's coherence, pacing, or character development. They can also give you feedback on aspects like dialogue, character growth, and general readability.

Characteristics of a Good Beta Reader or Critique Partner

When looking for a beta reader or critique partner, find someone who is a skilled reader and can provide helpful feedback. You should search for someone who can give you honest and unbiased opinions while still being supportive and respectful. It's also a good idea to find someone who is familiar with your type of writing or genre.

Tips for Finding Beta Readers and Critique Groups as a Writer

There are different methods to find beta readers for your writing. You could ask your acquaintances, family, or other writers if they would read your work and give you feedback. You could also search for beta reader communities on social media or online writing groups. Alternatively, you could hire a professional beta reader or editor to offer feedback on your writing.

How Many Beta Readers Should You Have?

The number of beta readers you need can depend on how long your book is and how much feedback you want. In general, it's a good idea to have at least three beta readers, but you don't want more than five or six because you don't want too many different opinions to work with. Having a few beta readers will give you enough feedback to work with, but not too much that it becomes too hard to handle.

Effective Communication with Beta Readers and Critique Groups

Communicating effectively with beta readers is essential to get the best feedback possible. Start by being clear about what type of feedback you need. Give them a list of specific questions or topics you want them to concentrate on. Additionally, make sure to establish clear expectations regarding timelines and deadlines. Lastly, be open to their feedback and ready to make changes to your writing based on their suggestions.

Types of Feedback to Expect from Critique Groups and Beta Readers

Critique groups and beta readers can give you diverse feedback, which includes recommendations for improvement, identification of plot holes or inconsistencies, and advice on character development and pacing. They can also provide overall thoughts on your writing style, tone, and voice. The kind of feedback you receive depends on the group or individual reader. Certain critique groups might concentrate more on the technical aspects of writing, while others might provide more subjective feedback.

Using Feedback to Improve Your Work as a Writer

When you get feedback from beta readers, take some time to go over it carefully. Look for common themes in their feedback and address any issues that many readers have mentioned. Take their feedback objectively and not be offended. Remember that their aim is to assist you in improving your writing, and their feedback can ultimately make your work better. Lastly, show your gratitude to your beta readers by thanking them for their effort and feedback. They've given their time and energy to help you improve, so it's essential to express your appreciation.

Best Practices for Using Feedback from Critique Groups and Beta Readers

Be receptive to all feedback while keeping in mind that not all feedback may be relevant or useful. Carefully assess the feedback you receive and determine if it matches your intentions for your work. If you need clarification on any particular points, don't hesitate to ask for it. Always show gratitude towards your critique group or beta readers for dedicating their time and effort to provide you with feedback.

Potential Downsides of Using Critique Groups or Beta Readers for Feedback on Your Writing

It's good to remember that people who give feedback on your writing aren't professional editors. Their opinions might not match your own style, and not all feedback will be useful to you. Make sure to think about where the feedback is coming from and if the person giving it has experience. Feedback can help you improve your writing, but be smart about which advice you take.

Dealing with Negative or Unhelpful Feedback from Beta Readers

Remember that not all feedback will be positive or helpful. If you receive negative feedback, try to stay open-minded and use it as an opportunity to learn and grow as a writer. However, if you receive feedback that is unhelpful or disrespectful, it's okay to politely thank the reader for their time and move on to another beta reader or critique partner.

Remember, It's up to you to decide which changes will make your story better, and which suggestions you can ignore.

76

Consider hiring a professional editor to give you objective feedback and help improve your writing

Getting help from a professional editor can significantly enhance the quality of your writing. They can spot errors and provide unbiased feedback on various aspects of your work, such as the plot, characters, pacing, and dialogue. They can also assist you in refining your writing style and ensuring that your work is easy to understand, concise, and captivating. Collaborating with an editor can also be an excellent opportunity for learning and growth as a writer.

Tips for Finding a Reliable and Experienced Editor

To find a professional editor, you can ask for suggestions from other writers or search online for freelance editors or editing services. You can also reach out to professional writing organizations for recommendations.

Factors to Consider When Selecting an Editor

When choosing an editor, find someone who has worked with your type of writing before and whom you feel comfortable working with. Check their qualifications and reputation, as well as their rates and schedule. Request samples of their work and feedback from previous clients. Consider their editing style and method to ensure that it meets your writing goals.

Understanding the Cost of Hiring an Editor

The price of an editor can differ based on various factors like the level of editing needed, the editor's experience, and the length of your writing. The cost can range from a few hundred dollars to several thousand. You should research and get estimates from different editors to find a price that suits your budget. Remember, hiring a professional editor can significantly enhance your writing quality and increase your chances of success as a writer.

The Writer's Role in the Editing Process

The amount of involvement you have in the editing process can change depending on your preference and the editor's method. Some editors may give you a detailed analysis and feedback, while others may make more significant alterations to your work. It's essential to speak openly with your editor about your expectations and preferences and be open to their suggestions and feedback. The end goal is to create the best possible version of your writing, and working with your editor can help you reach that goal.

77

Eliminating Unnecessary and Confusing Elements

To make your writing easy to understand, use short sentences and paragraphs that get straight to the point. Use active voice instead of passive, and avoid using complicated sentences or fancy words that might confuse your reader.

Sometimes, writing can become confusing or unnecessarily complicated due to complex plots, too much backstory, confusing world-building, or repetitive descriptions.

Identifying Unnecessary or Confusing Elements in Your Own Writing

To identify elements in your writing that are unnecessary or confusing, take a break and read your work with a critical eye. Ask yourself if each element is necessary for the story and whether it helps the reader understand the story better or not.

Strategies for Removing Unnecessary or Confusing Elements

To make your writing more effective, you can try to simplify your story by focusing on the main plot and characters and removing any elements that are not essential. Another option is to get feedback from someone else who can help identify confusing or unnecessary parts of your writing.

Balancing Clarity with Style and Creativity in Your Writing

It's possible to be both creative and clear in your writing. While using creative language and style can be great, make sure it doesn't affect the clarity of your writing. Before adding any creative element, ask yourself if it helps readers understand the story.

78

The Benefits of Reading Aloud

Reading your work out loud is a helpful way to find mistakes and make your writing better. When you read silently, your brain can skip over mistakes, but reading aloud makes you slow down and notice them.

Improving your writing by reading aloud

Reading your writing aloud can be very beneficial when editing for a few reasons.

Firstly, it can help you identify errors or awkward phrasing that you might not notice when reading silently. When you read out loud, you engage both your visual and auditory senses, which can make it easier to spot issues with sentence structure, grammar, and vocabulary and find places where you repeat the same words too much.

Moreover, reading your writing out loud can help you improve the rhythm and flow of your work. You can better understand how your sentences and paragraphs work together as a whole, and make adjustments accordingly. It can also help you identify where your writing might be too slow or too fast-paced.

Lastly, reading your work out loud can also help you get a better understanding of the tone and voice of your writing. You can hear how the words sound when put together and gain insight into how your writing will come across to readers.

Reading aloud during the writing process vs. Revisions

You can read your writing out loud at any stage, but it's especially helpful when you're making changes to your work. When you finish writing a draft, take some time to read it aloud and note the parts that need improvement. However, if you're having trouble writing well, reading your work aloud while you write can also be useful.

Technology and reading aloud: Can it help?

You can use various tools and apps to assist you in reading your work aloud. Text-to-speech programs are one option that can read your writing back to you. This can be especially useful if you are not able to read your work aloud yourself, or if you want to hear your writing from a different perspective. Some word-processing programs also have features that allow you to read your work aloud within the program.

Tips for effectively reading your work out loud

- Find a quiet place where you won't be disturbed.
- Speak clearly and with emotion, like you're talking to a group of people.
- Keep an eye on your speed and rhythm, and adjust if necessary.
- Take breaks if you get tired - reading aloud can be exhaust-

ing!
- Record yourself reading your work so you can listen to it later.

79

The Importance of Printing and Editing on Paper

Some writers like to edit their work on paper because it helps them spot mistakes and find areas where they can make improvements. When you're reading your work on a computer screen, your brain can get used to the text and you might miss errors that you would catch on paper. Also, when you print out your work, you can write notes and use highlighters to mark it up. This can make editing more fun and interactive!

What Errors Are Easier to Catch on Paper?

Some mistakes are easier to notice when you're editing on paper. For instance, you can see typos, spelling errors, and mistakes with punctuation and grammar more clearly. You might also notice problems with formatting, like spaces and margins that don't match. Plus, reading on paper can help you find places in your writing that need work, such as parts that are confusing, repetitive, or not fully developed.

Making the Most of Editing on Paper

When you're editing on paper, stay focused and take your time. Read your work carefully and make notes and marks as you go. And don't forget to transfer your changes back to your digital document once you're done!

The Downsides of Editing on Paper

Editing on paper has its advantages, but there are also some drawbacks to keep in mind. Printing out your work can take a lot of time and money, especially if you're working on a long piece. Plus, not all writers may find it comfortable or possible to edit on paper, especially those with disabilities. Lastly, some writers may find it hard to focus on the big picture when editing on paper, as they may get too caught up in small details.

Combining Paper Editing with Other Editing Methods

Editing on paper is useful, but it's not the only way to improve your writing. You can also read your work aloud, use editing software, or work with someone else to get feedback. By using a mix of methods that suit your writing style, you can catch more errors and make your writing better. Find what works for you!

80

Enhancing Your Editing Process with Online Tools and Editing Software

There are many helpful software and online tools for writers that can assist in editing. These tools have different functions, and they are designed to help writers improve their writing by correcting grammar, spelling, sentence structure, and style. Examples of such tools include Hemingway Editor, ProWritingAid, AutoCrit, and Grammarly.

Effectiveness of editing software and online tools in catching common mistakes

Although they are not flawless, these tools can be quite helpful in detecting typical errors that writers often make. They can spot spelling and grammar mistakes, assist in enhancing sentence structure, and suggest alternate word options. They can also pinpoint repeated words or phrases, which can help writers make their writing more effective and succinct.

Limitations of using editing software or online tools

Editing software and online tools are not infallible and

have some drawbacks. For instance, they may not detect all mistakes or provide the most appropriate solutions in every case. They can also lack the ability to comprehend the nuances of tone and context, which may lead to incorrect suggestions. Therefore, consider these tools as an additional aid to your personal editing approach, rather than depending on them entirely.

Incorporating editing software or online tools into the editing process

A useful method for using editing software or online tools is to use them as a final step in your editing process. After you've done your own revisions and edits, running your writing through these tools can help you catch any remaining errors or areas for improvement. When reviewing the suggestions made by the tool, use your own judgment to decide which changes are necessary and appropriate for your writing.

Can editing software or online tools replace the need for human editors?

While editing software and online tools are useful, they can't replace human editors entirely. A human editor can provide more personalized and detailed feedback that caters to your writing style and objectives. However, incorporating editing software or online tools can make the editing process more productive and cost-effective.

81

The Importance of Revising and Editing Your Work Thoroughly

It's difficult to give an exact amount since each writer and writing project is unique. However, I suggest aiming for a minimum of three rounds of revisions. The first round should address major issues like plot and character development. The second round should focus on language and style. The third round should be to identify any remaining errors.

Common Errors and Issues to Look for During the Revision Process

When you review your writing, you might find some problems like the story not matching or characters acting differently. Your sentences may sound strange or confusing, with too many extra words or repeating certain phrases too much. You may also notice that the story moves too slowly or the tone doesn't fit.

Remember, understand that no piece of writing is flawless, and revising doesn't mean you've made a mistake.

Approaching the Revision Process Systematically: Methods to Use

Before starting the revision process, some writers like to make a list or plan of things to check, like if they used certain words too much or if the story moves too fast or slow. Others prefer to revise in steps, maybe doing one chapter at a time or focusing on certain things to fix first. The key is to figure out what works best for you and how you write.

Knowing When Your Work is Ready for Submission: Signs to Look for

It's not always easy to know when your writing is completely done, but there comes a point where making more changes would do more harm than good. If you think you've addressed all the issues you or your readers found, and you feel that the story is as good as it can get, then it's likely time to send it in. Keep in mind that you can always keep making changes even after you submit, but eventually, you'll need to let it go and focus on new things.

<h1 style="text-align:center">82</h1>

Trimming the Fat: Removing Filler Words, Phrases and Passages from Your Writing

We all get fond of our writing, but be open to changing or shortening it to make it better. Sometimes, a sentence or paragraph can disrupt the story or theme and spoil the reader's enjoyment. By being open to editing, writers can make sure that their work is smooth, interesting, and serves the story well.

To do this, you need to know what kind of words and parts you can cut without harming your writing.

Filler words and phrases are words or phrases that don't add any meaning to your writing. People use them when they can't find the right words to express their thoughts. These words make your writing messy and less powerful.

Common Examples of Filler Words and Phrases in Writing

There are certain words and phrases that don't add anything meaningful to your writing and are just extra. Examples of these include "really," "very," "just," "in order to," "that," and "actually." These words and phrases can be taken out of a sentence without changing their meaning.

Filler words and phrases can make your writing seem un-professional and not well thought out.

Signs That Your Writing Needs to be Cut or Revised

There are a few ways to tell if a piece of writing needs to be revised. If a part of it doesn't fit with the story or doesn't add anything, that's a sign. Another sign is if the writing is awkward or the pacing is weird. And if you're having trouble making progress on it, that could mean it needs some changes.

Common Mistakes to Avoid When Cutting Unnecessary Words and Passages

People often make three errors. One is holding on too tightly to their words and being hesitant to improve them, even if it would make the writing better.

Another mistake is being overly focused on the word count, rather than the quality of the writing itself.

The last is not seeing how each part of the story is connected and fits together. Take a step back and see the writing as a whole to make sure it's working together and serving the story.

The Impact of Cutting Unnecessary Words and Passages on Writing Style

Removing words and parts that are not necessary can en-hance the quality of your writing by making it more direct and powerful. Your message will be clearer, and people will like how your writing is direct and to the point. It can also help you to refine your writing style by prompting you to concentrate on the most important parts of your work and removing anything that doesn't add value or meaning.

Techniques for Identifying Filler Words and Phrases in Your Writing

To find filler words and phrases in your writing, you can try reading it out loud. If you come across a word or phrase that doesn't add anything to the sentence, it's probably a filler. Another way is to look closely at each sentence and ask yourself if each word is needed to get your message across.

83

The Courage to Edit: Willingness to Rewrite or Remove Ineffective Sections

It can be challenging to make difficult choices, but remember that deleting or changing parts can make your story better. To find areas that need improvement, look for parts that are hard to read or don't make sense. You might also see that some scenes or characters don't really help the story or its message.

Signs that a Section Needs to be Cut or Rewritten

You should be aware of some warning signs, such as repetitive talking or doing the same thing, characters who don't change over time, or parts of the story that don't make sense or are irrelevant. If you get bored or uninterested when reading a certain part, it's likely that your readers will feel the same.

Ensuring Cutting or Rewriting Doesn't Negatively Impact the Story

When making changes to your story, remember the main idea and theme. Consider whether the section you're thinking of changing is necessary for the plot, character development, or the message you want to convey. You can also write a summary of the section before and after making changes to ensure it still fits well with the rest of the story.

Strategies for Rewriting Sections

Breaking down a section into smaller parts can make the process of rewriting or editing less daunting. Focusing on specific areas that need improvement can also make it easier to identify areas that may need changes. Additionally, you can try writing the section from a different point of view or tense to see if that improves the flow and pacing of the story.

Adding New Material vs Cutting or Rewriting: When is it Appropriate?

It's okay to add new material to your story if it improves the clarity or development of the story. But make sure that the new material doesn't disrupt the flow of the story or the pacing. Remember to keep your story's vision and theme in mind and adjust your changes accordingly.

84

Avoiding Over-Explaining or
Patronizing Your Readers

"Writing down" to the reader means making your writing too easy or simplistic that it no longer stimulates or interests the reader. This can happen when you explain a concept too much, use language that is too basic, or give all the answers to the reader without allowing them to think for themselves. In short, trust that your reader is smart enough to understand and follow along with your story without being overly directed.

Tips for avoiding over-explaining in writing

A good way to prevent over-explaining is by trusting your readers to understand your story without too much guidance. You can do this by showing important details through vivid descriptions and actions instead of just telling them. Additionally, having others review your work can help you avoid writing it down to your readers.

Importance of trusting the reader's intelligence in writing

Trusting your readers and letting them think for themselves

is crucial because it helps them connect more deeply with your story and characters. It also stimulates their critical thinking skills and encourages exploration, which can be very fulfilling. Additionally, it prevents your writing from being too simplistic or insulting to your readers and allows them to bring their unique perspectives and experiences, which makes for a more complex and interesting reading experience.

Balancing information and interpretation in writing

Finding the right balance between giving enough information and allowing room for interpretation can be tricky, but keeping readers engaged and challenged. One way to do this is to provide some background information to help readers understand the characters and setting, but leave some things open to interpretation. You can also use dialogue and action to convey important information, which can make the story more engaging. Lastly, consider the pacing of your story and how much information you're revealing at once, as this can affect how your readers engage with your writing.

85

The Importance of Editing with Both the Big Picture and Details in Mind

Finding a balance between looking at the big picture and paying attention to the smaller details is key. While understanding the story's overall structure, theme, and characters is important, it's also necessary to focus on the details that give your story personality. This could include aspects like sentence structure, word selection, and grammar.

What Are Big Picture Elements in Writing Editing?
When considering the big picture, pay attention to elements like the speed at which the story unfolds, the way characters speak and act the effectiveness of the setting, and the overall feeling and atmosphere of the piece. These things should work together to create a story that is interesting and makes sense.

Importance of Considering Big Picture While Editing Writing?
When you focus on the bigger picture, you can ensure that your story is not only interesting but also meaningful and

effective. By looking at the overall story, you can identify and fix any issues, like confusing parts or parts that don't make sense. This can help make sure that every part of your story is important and moves the story forward.

Tips for Keeping the Big Picture in Mind While Editing Writing.

There are several useful techniques you can use to stay focused on the big picture of your writing. One is to make an outline or a story map before you start writing, so you have a clear idea of where your story is going. Another is to take breaks while editing so that you can come back to your work with fresh eyes and a clear head. Lastly, you can seek feedback from others to gain an outside perspective and make sure that your big-picture elements are working effectively.

86

Beyond Grammar and Spelling: Editing for Clarity, Coherence, and More

When you edit your work for clarity and coherence, you're making sure that your writing is clear and easy to understand for your reader. This includes making sure that your sentences and paragraphs are organized in a logical way, and that your ideas flow smoothly from one to the next.

Tips for Ensuring Clarity and Coherence in Your Writing

A helpful technique for editing your work is to read it aloud, which can reveal any awkward or unclear phrasing and help you assess the flow of ideas. Another approach is to ask someone else to read your work and provide feedback on its clarity and coherence.

Common Mistakes to Avoid When Editing for Clarity and Coherence

Readers may not always understand what a writer is trying to convey, so it's necessary to make ideas clear and easy to follow. Avoid using complex or difficult sentence structures that can make the writing harder to comprehend.

Benefits of Editing for Clarity and Coherence

If your writing is easy to understand, your readers will be able to follow your ideas and stay interested in your work. This can make your writing more effective and impactful.

Differences Between Editing for Clarity and Coherence and Editing for Grammar and Spelling

When editing your writing, check for both clarity and coherence as well as grammar and spelling. While grammar and spelling ensuring that each sentence is correct, clarity and coherence ensure that the writing makes sense as a whole and that the ideas are easy to understand for the reader. Prioritize both aspects to make sure your writing is effective and engaging.

87

Willingness to Experiment and Take Risks

Take risks when revising your writing because it can lead to making your story better. If you are too afraid to take risks, you may miss out on opportunities to make significant changes that could make your writing stand out. By taking risks, you can be more creative and explore new ideas that can improve your writing and make it more memorable.

Examples of risks writers can take during revision

Writers can take many risks during the revision process, such as changing the story's perspective, plot, characters, or writing style. They can even take the story in a completely different direction than planned. Although these risks may not always succeed, they can help writers improve and develop their skills.

Benefits of taking risks during revision

Being adventurous during revision can make a writer's work more captivating, thrilling, and memorable. By experimenting and taking risks, a writer can produce a piece that is distinct and remarkable. Moreover, taking risks can unveil new abilities and drawbacks in writing, which can lead to further progress and advancement as a writer.

Potential pitfalls of taking risks during revision

Although taking risks during revision can lead to significant improvements in your writing, Remember that not all risks will pay off. Some may result in a weaker story, or may not resonate with readers as intended. Additionally, risk-taking can be time-consuming and require a lot of effort to implement. Approach risk-taking with an open mind and willingness to learn from any challenges or setbacks that may arise.

Balancing risks and maintaining the integrity of the story during revision

To balance taking risks with maintaining the integrity of your story, stay true to your creative vision and be mindful of the story's essence. When experimenting with new ideas, consider whether they align with the story's overall theme and tone. It's also helpful to seek feedback from beta readers or critique partners to ensure that your risks enhance, rather than detract from, the story. This approach can help you strike the right balance between taking creative risks and maintaining the integrity of your work.

88

Making Bold Changes: Willingness to Revise Significantly for the Betterment of the Story

It can be scary to make major changes to a story, but the goal is always to improve the writing. If you feel that something isn't working, whether it's the plot or characters, it may be necessary to make significant changes. One way to determine this is to seek feedback from beta readers or critique partners. If they consistently identify the same issues, it may be worth making big changes. It can be hard to let go of certain aspects of your writing, but remember that no writing is perfect, and making changes can ultimately improve the overall quality of your work.

Examples of significant changes that can improve a story

Making significant changes to a story means altering important elements such as the perspective, ending, or characters. These changes should always serve the purpose of improving the story and enhancing the reader's experience. Keep in mind the overall story and characters when making significant changes and avoid making changes just for the sake of it.

Avoiding changes that harm the story or characters

To avoid making changes that could negatively impact your story, stay true to your original vision and consider whether any changes serve the story and characters in a meaningful way. Seek feedback from others to ensure that any changes you make are improving the story rather than hurting it. Remember that your vision for the story is important and should not be compromised.

Balancing the desire to make changes with staying true to the original vision

Finding a balance between making necessary changes to improve your story and staying true to your vision can be challenging. To achieve this balance, it's essential to keep your overall vision for the story in mind while editing. When considering changes, evaluate whether they align with the story's themes, message, and tone. Also, be willing to compromise and explore creative solutions that maintain the story's integrity. Remember, the goal is to create the best possible version of your story while satisfying the needs of your audience.

89

Sticking to the Plan: Avoiding Major Story Changes During Editing and Saving Them for Revisions

Although it may be tempting to make significant changes to your story as you write, it's usually better to wait until the revision stage. This is because revisions involve a more comprehensive reworking of the manuscript, while editing is primarily concerned with refining the existing text.

Difference between editing and revising

When you edit your manuscript, you are making small improvements to the language, style, and organization to make it easier to read and more interesting for your audience. You may correct mistakes in grammar and spelling, adjust sentence structure, and ensure your writing flows smoothly. During revision, you focus on the big picture of the story and characters. You may make significant changes to the plot, character development, or themes to make your story more coherent and meaningful.

Identifying minor and major changes

Minor changes are ones that don't have a big impact on the story, such as small edits to a character's dialogue or name. Major changes, on the other hand, can greatly affect the plot, characters, or themes of the story.

When to save major changes for revisions

It's best to wait until you have completed your entire manuscript before making any significant changes. This will allow you to have a clear understanding of the story and ensure that any changes you make are consistent with the rest of the book, without causing any issues down the line.

Examples of minor changes

Minor changes could refer to small adjustments that do not significantly impact the story, such as correcting errors in grammar or spelling, enhancing sentence structure to make the text more readable, or clearing up passages that are difficult to understand.

Balancing changes with preserving the original vision of the story

When you're making changes to your story, consider how they align with your overall vision for the piece. Ask yourself why you're making a particular change and if it fits into the big picture. If you're uncertain, take a step back and give yourself some time to reflect before proceeding. You can also seek feedback from beta readers or a writing group to get an outside perspective on your changes.

90

Finding Closure: Knowing When to End the Revision Process and Submit Your Work

It's common for writers to have difficulty determining when to stop revising their work. To help with this, consider the purpose of your writing. Are you writing for your own enjoyment or are you hoping to have your work published? If it's for personal satisfaction, you can revise as much as you want until you're happy with the final product. But if you plan to submit your work for publication, be mindful of deadlines and submission guidelines.

Signs that a piece of writing is ready to be submitted

When deciding if your writing is ready for submission, there are a few things to consider. Firstly, make sure you have a clear idea of the story you want to tell and that all the writing elements work towards that goal. Secondly, ensure that your writing is polished and free from any spelling or grammatical errors. Thirdly, seek feedback from other writers or beta readers and make necessary revisions to your final draft. Lastly, feel confident and proud of your writing before submitting it.

Avoiding the trap of endless revision

To avoid getting stuck in the cycle of constant revision, you can set a deadline for yourself and create a schedule for making revisions leading up to that date. You can also seek feedback from other writers or editors early in the revision process to get a better idea of what needs to be changed and avoid endless tweaking.

Potential drawbacks of submitting work too soon

Sending your writing for submission before it's ready can be damaging to your career as a writer. Revise and refine your writing before submitting it. Submitting it too soon can also cause missed opportunities. You may not be able to submit it to a better publication or miss out on a chance for a higher payment if you hurry to submit your work.

Balancing the desire for perfection with the need to submit

Finding the right balance between striving for excellence and submitting your work can be challenging. Remember that perfection is unattainable, so set high standards for yourself but be realistic. Recognize when your writing has reached its full potential and don't let the desire for perfection prevent you from sharing your work with others. Remember that submitting your writing is an important part of the process.

VI

Publishing And Marketing

91

Research the publishing industry and agents

Authors have various options to publish their books, including traditional publishing, self-publishing, and hybrid publishing. In traditional publishing, an author submits their manuscript to a publishing house or literary agent who will take care of the editing, design, printing, and distribution. In self-publishing, the author handles all these steps independently, while hybrid publishing is a mix of both.

Understanding the Different Types of Publishing

There are mainly two ways to get a book published: traditional publishing and self-publishing.

In traditional publishing, the author submits their manuscript to a publishing house or literary agent, who takes care of editing, printing, marketing, and distribution of the book. The author typically gets an advance payment and a portion of the book's sales. Self-publishing, on the other hand, is when the author is responsible for all aspects of publishing, including editing, marketing, and distribution.

This means that the author pays for everything upfront and receives all profits from the book's sales

Pros and Cons of Traditional Publishing vs Self-Publishing
Traditional publishing can give you access to industry experts and established publishing networks, potentially leading to a wider distribution and higher sales. But it can be a challenging and competitive process with longer wait times and lower royalties. Self-publishing lets you keep creative control, earn higher royalties, and get your book published more quickly. However, you'll need to handle all publishing tasks yourself and may not have access to professional resources.

Determining the Right Publishing Option for Your Book and Goals
Deciding which publishing option is best for your book comes down to your goals for your work. If you want to reach a broad audience and gain more exposure, traditional publishing may be the right choice. However, if you prefer full control over your book and want to publish it quickly, self-publishing might be the way to go. A hybrid approach can provide you with the benefits of both options.

Key Factors to Consider When Researching Publishing Options
When considering your publishing options, you should think about several things, such as the type of book you have written, who your readers are, how much money you have to spend, when you want your book to be available, and your ultimate objectives. Additionally, you should investigate the reputation and experience of any potential publishers or agents and

examine their marketing and distribution strategies.

Researching and Identifying Reputable Publishers or Agents

To ensure you find reputable publishers or agents, do some research. Find publishers or agents who have experience and success with authors in your genre. Check out their submission guidelines to confirm they're a good match for your manuscript. Many online resources, like the Writer's Market, can assist you in finding reputable publishers or agents.

Authors can access numerous resources to assist with researching publishing options. These resources include online writing communities, publishing directories, industry websites, and literary agents. Joining writing communities or attending writing conferences are additional ways to connect with authors and industry professionals.

What to Look for in an Agent or Publisher for Your Book

When searching for an agent or publisher, it's essential to ensure they are compatible with your writing style. Consider their track record of success in publishing works similar to yours, as well as their industry reputation. Additionally, assess whether their communication style aligns with your own and if they appear to be a good fit for you as an individual.

Common Misconceptions about the Publishing Industry

There are some misunderstandings about the publishing industry. One of them is that traditional publishing is the only way to succeed in the industry. Although traditional publishing can provide greater exposure and success, self-publishing has also become a reputable and successful option in recent years.

Another common misconception is that self-publishing is an effortless way to make quick money. However, self-publishing requires a lot of effort, time, and commitment to succeed.

Making an Informed Decision About Your Publishing Option

Before deciding on a publishing option, it's essential to think about your goals and what you can afford. Traditional publishing may be the way to go if you want to benefit from an established publisher's support and resources, while self-publishing may be a better option if you desire full control over the process and the potential for higher earnings.

Take into account your available time and resources and carefully consider the advantages and disadvantages of each option. Speaking to other authors who have gone through the traditional publishing and self-publishing process can also be helpful. Ultimately, the best choice will depend on your particular situation and aspirations

Red Flags to Watch Out for When Researching Agents or Publishers

Be cautious when researching agents or publishers. Watch out for those who ask for payment upfront or make unrealistic promises. Also, be mindful of negative reviews and any history of unethical practices.

How Many Agents or Publishers Should You Submit to at Once?

To increase your chances of acceptance, it's best to submit your work to a handful of agents or publishers at a time rather than submitting to all of them at once. This way, you can evaluate the feedback you receive and make any necessary changes before submitting more. I suggest beginning with 5-10 agents or publishers to start.

Tailoring Your Submissions to Increase Your Chances of Acceptance

Adhere to the specific submission guidelines of each agent or publisher, and you can do this by researching their require-ments and following them diligently. Additionally, tailor your query letter to each agent or publisher, demonstrating that you've researched their work and understand their interests. Finally, ensure that your manuscript is of high quality and thoroughly edited before submitting it.

92

Don't be afraid to try new marketing strategies or approaches to see what works best for your book.

It's essential for authors to experiment with new marketing strategies because the publishing industry and readers' tastes are always evolving. What was effective for another author or book may not work for you, so test various methods to discover what suits you and your book best. Moreover, exploring new techniques can help you connect with fresh audiences and broaden your readership.

Examples of New Marketing Strategies for Authors to Try

Authors have many innovative marketing strategies available to them, including using TikTok to showcase their writing process, partnering with other authors or influencers to run book giveaways or joint promotions, or creating engaging multimedia content such as book trailers. Keep up with the latest social media trends and platforms and try out different content types like podcasts, webinars, or virtual events to expand your audience

How to Track the Success of a Marketing Strategy as an Author

To measure the success of a marketing strategy, you can keep an eye on book sales and downloads, and track engagement and traffic on your website or social media pages. You can also use surveys or feedback forms to find out how readers feel about your book or marketing efforts. Set specific goals and metrics for success before implementing a new strategy so that you can accurately evaluate its effectiveness and determine your next steps.

Determining How Long to Give a Marketing Strategy Before Evaluating its Success

Be patient when evaluating the effectiveness of a marketing strategy. Give the strategy enough time to gain traction and gather data, which usually takes a few weeks to a month. However, some strategies may take longer to see results, stay persistent and not give up too soon.

Examples of Successful Marketing Strategies Used by Authors

Authors have implemented various marketing strategies with success, including building an engaging online presence, partnering with bloggers or book reviewers for interviews and reviews, hosting virtual book events, and promoting their books through targeted advertisements or sponsored content on social media platforms. Try out different approaches and find what works best for your book and audience.

93

Consider self-publishing if traditional publishing doesn't work out

Self-publishing is a good choice for authors who have not succeeded in traditional publishing. The main advantage is that you have total control over the publishing process, from editing to pricing. You also get to keep a greater percentage of your earnings. Nonetheless, there are drawbacks, such as the need to manage all aspects of marketing and distribution, which can be difficult and time-consuming.

Is Self-Publishing Right for Your Book? Consider These Factors

Deciding whether to self-publish depends on what you want to achieve with your book. If you're looking to make a profit or establish a writing career, self-publishing may not be the best choice. However, if your priority is to share your work and engage with readers, self-publishing can be a great option. Additionally, the genre of your book can also influence whether self-publishing is a good fit, as certain genres tend to do better in the self-publishing market.

Common Mistakes to Avoid as a New Self-Published Author

Many new self-published authors make the mistake of not dedicating enough time to editing and revising their work. Additionally, some authors overlook the importance of investing in a professional cover design and formatting. Lastly, some authors do not adequately market their books, which can make it challenging to attract readers.

Effective Marketing Strategies for Self-Published Books

When it comes to marketing your self-published book, there are many tactics to consider, but audience-building is key. This involves establishing a robust social media presence, creating an email list, and collaborating with book bloggers and reviewers. Additionally, running ads on platforms such as Amazon and Facebook, as well as reaching out to book clubs and local bookstores can be effective strategies.

Building an Audience as a Self-Published Author: Tips and Strategies

Establishing an audience requires dedication and patience, but there are a few steps you can take to get started. Begin by creating a robust online presence that includes a website, social media accounts, and an email list. Also, connect with other writers and readers who share your genre and offer them free samples or book excerpts to encourage them to read your work. Additionally, consider participating in book giveaways or other promotional events to expose your book to more potential readers.

94

Build a platform and connect with readers through social media and blogging

To succeed in today's market, authors need to have a platform and engage with readers. This helps to build a relationship with readers, increase visibility, and ultimately sell more books. By having a platform, authors can connect with readers, showcase their work, and establish themselves as authorities in their genres.

Effective Ways to Build a Platform and Connect with Readers
There are various ways to create a platform and connect with readers effectively. Some of the commonly used techniques are developing a website or blog, communicating with readers on social media, attending book fairs and literary events, and providing giveaways or exclusive content to email subscribers. Identify what resonates with you and your readers, and frequently interact with them in a significant manner.

Using Social Media and Blogging to Reach a Wider Audience

Social media and blogging are great ways for authors to reach out to a larger audience. By using platforms like Twitter, Instagram, and Facebook, you can connect with readers, share information about your work, and build a community around your brand. Blogging is also a great way to express your thoughts and provide valuable content to your readers. When used effectively, social media and blogging can help you attract new readers and keep your existing audience interested.

Common Mistakes to Avoid When Building a Platform as an Author

One mistake that authors often make is trying to maintain a presence on too many platforms simultaneously. Concentrate on the platforms where your readers are most active and where you can connect with them most effectively. Another mistake is having an unclear brand or message, which can perplex readers and make it difficult for them to relate to you. Lastly, authors should avoid being too self-promotional and instead concentrate on providing valuable content to their readers through their platforms.

Best Practices and Strategies for Building a Platform as an Author

Many authors have found success by following certain best practices and strategies. These include maintaining consistency in your branding and message, regularly interacting with your audience, delivering valuable content, and collaborating with other authors or industry professionals. While it's crucial to experiment and find what works best for you, adopting these best practices can significantly improve your chances of success.

<h1 style="text-align:center">95</h1>

Develop a strong author brand and stick to it across all platforms

An author brand is like a personality or identity that sets you apart from other writers. It includes your writing style, the types of books you write, how you present yourself online, and how you market your work. Your brand should communicate a clear message to your readers and help you establish a unique identity as an author.

Importance of Having a Strong Author Brand

Creating a powerful author brand can assist you in becoming a successful author and developing a devoted readership. By clearly defining your brand and promoting it consistently across all channels, you can build a distinctive and unforgettable image for yourself and your writing. This can assist readers in remembering your name and looking for your books in the future.

Defining Your Author Brand

To define your author brand, you need to identify what

makes you a strong writer, understand your ideal readers, and decide on the tone and message you want to convey. Consider what themes and values are important to you and show up in your writing. Think about the type of reader you want to appeal to and what they are looking for in a book. With a clear understanding of your brand, you can create a consistent message and image across all platforms.

Examples of Successful Author Brands

Many successful authors have established their brands over time. Stephen King is known for his horror and suspense stories often set in small towns with supernatural themes. J.K. Rowling is famous for the Harry Potter series, which emphasizes friendship, bravery, and magic. Neil Gaiman is known for his fusion of fantasy and mythology. These authors have created a clear message and image that has connected with readers and helped them become popular and successful.

Ensuring Consistency Across All Platforms

To build a strong brand, maintain consistency. Develop a style guide that covers your brand message, tone, voice, and visual elements. Utilize this guide to create a consistent appearance and atmosphere across all your platforms, such as your website, social media, and book covers. Ensure that your messaging aligns with your brand values and remains consistent. Regularly evaluate and refresh your brand to keep it current and interesting.

Communicating Your Author Brand Effectively

To communicate your brand effectively, be authentic and engage with your audience. You can use social media to interact with readers, post updates about your writing, and create content that aligns with your brand values. Collaborating with other authors or brands can also help you reach a wider audience. By promoting your brand consistently and engaging with your audience, you can become a successful and memorable author.

96

Use social media and online platforms to build your audience and promote your work

Social media and online platforms are great tools for authors to connect with readers and market their work. The first step is to select a few platforms that you can handle efficiently, rather than trying to be active on every platform. Twitter, Facebook and Instagram are some of the most popular platforms for authors to use.

Building a Strong Social Media Presence as an Author: Tips and Advice

To build a strong social media presence as an author, you need to put in time and effort. First, find out where your target audience is most active and create a brand image that's consistent across all platforms. Develop a content strategy that will appeal to your audience, such as sharing behind-the-scenes looks at your writing process, and make sure to post on a regular basis.

You should also interact with your followers by responding to their comments and messages and engaging with other users' posts. Additionally, using hashtags can help increase the visibility of your content to potential readers.

How to effectively promote your book without being spammy

To effectively promote your book on social media, you should aim to create a mix of content that includes promotion and other interesting content for your followers. Some ways to promote your book can be by sharing sneak peeks, updates on your writing journey, running giveaways or offering exclusive content to your followers. However, it's essential to strike a balance between self-promotion and sharing other valuable content with your audience.

The Best Social Media Platforms for Authors: Which Ones to Use

Choosing the best social media platforms for authors largely depends on their readers and genre. Some common social media platforms for authors are Twitter, Instagram, Facebook, and Goodreads. Twitter is ideal for brief updates and connecting with other writers and industry experts. Instagram is suitable for sharing visual content like book covers and behind-the-scenes photos. Facebook is useful for creating a community around your work and interacting with readers, and Goodreads is a social network that specifically focuses on readers and book recommendations.

Other online platforms to consider for promoting your work

In addition to social media, there are other websites you can use to market your book, including Goodreads, BookBub, and Wattpad. Starting a blog or podcast about writing or your book's subject matter is another great way to reach potential readers.

Common mistakes to avoid when using social media to promote your work

Many authors make the mistake of only using social media to promote their books and not talking to their readers. Another mistake is being too negative or starting arguments, which can make people not want to read their book. Always be polite and professional when using social media.

Engaging with Readers on Social Media: Strategies for Authors

Interacting with your readers on social media can help you gain loyal followers and promote your work. You can engage with your audience by answering their comments and messages, holding contests and giveaways, organizing Q&A sessions, and sharing exclusive content. Be authentic and true to yourself in your interactions with readers. Don't hesitate to show your personality and share personal anecdotes or insights into your writing process.

The key to successful social media promotion is to be creative and find ways to connect with your audience in an engaging way.

Social Media Marketing: Do's and Don'ts to Keep in Mind

To succeed in social media marketing as an author, it's essential to consistently maintain your branding and posting schedule, engage with your followers, and share interesting content that your audience can relate to. Conduct yourself professionally, be respectful and avoid being too promotional or spammy.

Don't fall into the trap of using clickbait or engaging in controversial topics that may alienate your audience. Additionally, it's vital to be aware of your personal information and privacy settings while sharing on social media.

Measuring the Success of Your Social Media and Online Platform Efforts as an Author

Measuring the success of your social media and online platform efforts is essential to determine what works best for your audience. To track your success, you can monitor your follower count, engagement rates, website traffic, and sales from social media. Set specific goals and track your progress towards achieving them. This way, you can identify what's working and what needs improvement.

Social Media Posting Frequency for Authors: How Often Should Authors Be Posting on Social Media to Promote Their Work?

Posting content on social media regularly is important for authors, but ensure that the content is of high quality and engaging. It's better to have fewer but high-quality posts that attract and retain readers' attention than to have many low-quality posts. Therefore, authors should aim to post regularly, whether that's once a day or a few times a week while prioritizing quality over quantity.

Examples of Authors Who Have Successfully Used Social Media: Case Studies of Authors Who Have Used Social Media to Promote Their Work Successfully

Liane Moriarty is a great example of an author who effec-tively uses social media to connect with her readers and share updates on her writing process. Another successful author in this regard is John Green, who has a large following on YouTube and shares book recommendations, Q&A sessions, and other writing-related content. Both authors have success-fully used social media to establish a strong connection with their readers and promote their work.

97

Engage with your readers and respond to reviews and feedback

When you take the time to respond to reviews and feedback, it demonstrates to your readers that you appreciate and respect their opinions. This can help establish a rapport with your readers, build trust, and give you valuable insight into their interests and preferences.

Dealing with Negative Reviews or Feedback

Negative feedback and reviews can be challenging to handle, but keep in mind that they can offer valuable insights. It's essential to take the time to read and comprehend the feedback, noting any trends or concerns readers are expressing. Use this feedback to improve your writing and address any issues. When responding to negative reviews, always remain courteous and professional, even if you don't entirely agree with the criticism.

Using Reader Feedback to Improve Your Writing

Getting feedback from readers is helpful in understanding

their preferences and opinions about your writing. Look out for any recurring themes or issues that readers may be pointing out and use them to improve your writing. You may also want to consider reaching out to a select group of readers to get more specific feedback by doing beta reads or conducting surveys.

Tips for Responding to Reviews and Feedback Professionally
Here are some suggestions for responding to reviews and feedback in a professional manner:

- Express your gratitude for the reviewer's time and effort in reading and reviewing your book.
- Acknowledge the feedback, even if you don't fully agree with it.
- Maintain a professional and polite tone in your response.
- Avoid becoming defensive or getting into arguments with reviewers.
- If the reviewer had a negative experience with your book, offer to make things right.

98

Use cover art and book descriptions to sell your book

Your cover art and book description are critical to grabbing readers' attention and encouraging them to explore your book. They are often the first things potential readers will see when looking for books online or in a bookstore. Your cover art should be attractive, and memorable, and reflect the tone and genre of your book. Your book description should be engaging and highlight the unique aspects of your story to give readers a reason to read it.

Key Elements to Include in a Book Description

When creating your book description, include a hook that grabs the reader's attention, a brief summary of the plot, and some details about the main character(s) or setting. If you have any positive reviews or endorsements, you can also include those, as well as any relevant genre or theme keywords that can help your book show up in searches. But be careful not to give away too much of the story. You want to create an interesting and accurate summary that makes readers eager to learn more.

Tips for Creating Effective Cover Art

Creating an effective cover for your book can be done in various ways, but some tips that may help are to choose a visual element that represents your book's genre or theme, use typography that is easy to read and use colors that complement each other. You may also want to check out other books in your genre to see what works and what doesn't. Remember that your cover will appear in different formats and platforms, so ensure it looks great in all of them.

Common Mistakes to Avoid When Creating Cover Art and Book Descriptions

There are some mistakes that can harm your book's chances of getting attention. Common ones include using generic or unrelated images or fonts, having a description that is either too vague or too detailed and not checking for typos or errors. Also, avoid trying to appeal to everyone and instead create something that specifically targets your intended audience.

Recommended Resources and Tools for Creating Effective Cover Art and Book Descriptions

You can find many helpful tools for creating great cover art and book descriptions. Canva is a free online tool that can assist you in making attractive designs and graphics. Reedsy has a book description generator that can help you get started with writing the description. It's also useful to study other books in your genre to understand what works and what doesn't. Remember, creating an effective cover and book description is crucial in getting your book noticed and appealing to potential readers. Take the time to create something that represents your book well and grabs the attention of your target audience.

99

Use a professional editor or cover designer to create a polished finished product

It's a great idea to hire a professional editor and cover designer because they can greatly improve the quality of your book and how it's received by readers. An editor can help you make your writing better by improving its structure, clarity, and flow, and by giving you feedback on important elements like characters and plot. A cover designer can create a cover that looks amazing and accurately represents your book's style and genre, which can attract potential readers.

Finding a Good Editor or Cover Designer

If you're looking for a good editor or cover designer, there are a few ways to go about it. You could ask other writers or writing groups for suggestions, search for freelance professionals on websites like Upwork or Freelancer, or look for specialized editing or design services online. Just make sure to read reviews and do your research before making a final decision.

What to Look for When Hiring an Editor or Cover Designer

If you're hiring an editor, find someone who has worked on books in your genre before and who gets your ideas for the book. You should also look for someone who is professional, easy to talk to, and responds to your messages in a timely manner. If you're hiring a cover designer, you should find someone who has a portfolio of covers that you admire and who understands the style and tone of your book.

Expected Cost for Editor and Cover Designer Services

The cost of editing and cover design can vary greatly depending on what you need and the experience of the professional you hire. For editing, the cost can range from a few hundred to several thousand dollars depending on the length of your book and what kind of editing you require. For cover design, you can expect to pay anywhere from a few hundred to a few thousand dollars depending on how complex the design is and how experienced the designer is.

Tips for Effective Collaboration with Editor or Cover Designer

Good communication is essential when collaborating with an editor or cover designer. Have a clear understanding of what work needs to be done and when it needs to be done. Additionally, be open to feedback and suggestions and show respect for the editor or designer's knowledge and time. Lastly, make sure to pay them promptly for their hard work.

100

Build relationships with other writers and industry professionals

For authors, establishing connections with other writers and industry professionals can be highly beneficial regardless of their experience level. It can help you gain insights and enhance your writing skills, while also leading to new opportunities and partnerships.

Moreover, having a solid network of peers and contacts in the writing community can offer emotional support and motivation throughout your writing journey. Although writing can often be a solitary pursuit, linking with others who comprehend the ups and downs of the process can make a huge difference

Effective Ways to Build Relationships in the Writing Community

There are many ways to make connections with other writers and industry professionals. Attending writing conferences and workshops can help you meet other writers and learn from experienced professionals. Joining writing groups or organizations, either online or in person, can also connect you with other writers who share your interests and goals.

You can also use social media platforms like Twitter, Facebook, and Instagram to build relationships in the writing community. Many writers and industry professionals are active on social media and engage with others regularly. But remember to approach interactions with respect and professionalism, and avoid spamming or overly promotional behaviour.

How Building Relationships with Industry Professionals Can Help Authors

Connecting with industry professionals, like editors, agents, and publishers can help authors find new opportunities and understand the publishing industry better. However, keep in mind that building relationships with these professionals requires patience and hard work. Treat their time and knowledge with respect, and aim to build relationships that benefit both parties, not just your own career.

Common Mistakes to Avoid When Building Relationships in the Writing Community

One mistake to avoid when building relationships in the writing community is only reaching out to others when you need something. Instead, focus on building authentic connections and offering value to others whenever you can. Additionally, respect other people's boundaries and not be too aggressive in your interactions. Lastly, be respectful and open-minded towards others, even if they don't share your views, and avoid getting into heated arguments or behaving in a toxic manner.

Best Practices and Strategies for Building Relationships in the Writing Community

A great strategy to build relationships is to approach them with a mindset of kindness and helpfulness. Offer your assistance to others in the community by providing feedback, sharing their work, or giving words of encouragement.

Consistency and persistence are also crucial to building strong relationships. Attend conferences, join groups, and engage with others on social media regularly to establish connections over time.

Remember that building relationships are not just about advancing your own career, but also about contributing to a supportive and encouraging community for all writers

101

Keep learning and improving your craft to keep readers coming back

Continuous learning and improvement are crucial for authors who want to succeed in the long run. Writing is a skill that requires constant practice and honing to achieve its full potential. By continuously learning and improving, you can keep your writing interesting and engaging, and keep your readers engaged. Keep up with the latest trends and techniques in the publishing industry to stay ahead of the game.

Effective Ways to Continue Learning and Improving Your Writing Craft

There are several ways to improve your writing skills. You can start by reading widely and analyzing the work of other writers to learn different writing styles and techniques that you can apply to your own writing. Additionally, taking writing classes or workshops either in person or online can help you learn from experienced writers and receive feedback on your work. Finally, make writing a regular habit by setting aside time to practice writing every day or week, no matter how brief the session may be. Consistently practicing your craft can help you improve and refine your writing style.

Using Feedback from Readers and Reviews to Improve Your Writing

Hearing from your readers through reviews can be very helpful for improving your writing. Listen to their opinions, both the good and the bad. Take note of what they liked and disliked, and use this information to help you with your future writing.

But keep in mind, not all feedback is created equal. Some readers may not have the same preferences as your target audience, or may not understand your artistic vision fully. It's up to you to decide which feedback to take seriously and which to ignore

Common Mistakes to Avoid When Improving Your Writing Craft

One mistake to avoid when trying to improve your writing craft is to be overly critical of yourself. Be honest with yourself, but don't let self-doubt or fear hold you back. Another mistake is to focus solely on the technical aspects of writing, such as grammar, without giving enough attention to storytelling and character development. Avoid getting too comfortable in your writing and keep challenging yourself to try new things and explore different styles and genres.

Resources and Tools to Help with Learning and Improving Your Writing Craft

You can find lots of resources and tools to help improve your writing skills. For example, online writing communities like

Critique Circle and Scribophile offer opportunities for feedback and support. Grammarly and Hemingway are websites that can help you improve your writing mechanics.

There are also many books and courses that focus on various writing topics like plot, character development, and dialogue. Some popular books on writing craft are "On Writing" by Stephen King, "Bird by Bird" by Anne Lamott, and "Plot & Structure" by James Scott Bell.

Moreover, there are many writing communities and critique groups that you can join to get feedback on your work and connect with other writers. Remember to find resources and tools that work best for your writing style

102

Use keywords and SEO to help your book get discovered online

Keywords are the words or phrases people use to find things online. For books, using the right keywords in your book's information can help make sure it shows up in search results when people are looking for books like yours. SEO is about making sure your website or other online content shows up high in search results when people search for relevant keywords.

Determining the Best Keywords for Your Book

To find the best keywords for your book, try to put yourself in the shoes of someone who might be searching for a book like yours. Think about what words or phrases they might use when searching online. If your book is a romance novel, you could try using keywords such as "romance novel," "love story," or "relationship drama." Additionally, you can use tools like Google's Keyword Planner to help you find relevant keywords to include in your book's metadata

Optimizing Your Book's Metadata for Better Search Results

To optimize your book's metadata, focus on a few important elements. Firstly, ensure that your book's title and subtitle accurately describe what your book is about and include relevant keywords. Secondly, write an engaging book description that also includes keywords and gives readers a clear idea of what to expect. Finally, ensure that your book's metadata is consistent across all platforms where it is listed, such as Amazon or Barnes & Noble.

Tips for Using Keywords and SEO Effectively

Here are some helpful tips:

· Avoid using too many keywords in your book's metadata or content, as it may negatively affect your search rankings.

· Make sure that your book's content is engaging and valuable to readers.

· Utilize social media and other online platforms to promote your book and attract readers to your website or other online content.

• Stay informed about changes to search algorithms and adapt your SEO strategy accordingly to stay ahead of the game

103

Consider creating a book trailer or other multimedia content to promote your work

A book trailer is like a mini-movie that showcases your book in an engaging way. It's a great way to get readers interested in your book and give them a sneak peek of what they can expect.

Exploring Other Forms of Multimedia Content to Promote Your Book

Besides book trailers, there are many other types of multimedia content you can make to advertise your book, such as:

- Interviews with you as the author or Q&A sessions
- Podcast episodes or audio clips
- Character sketches or illustrations
- Social media graphics or memes
- Live readings or performances
- Behind-the-scenes videos, like footage of your writing or

editing process.

Creating Budget-Friendly Book Trailers and Multimedia Content

Creating multimedia content to promote your book doesn't have to break the bank. If you're making a book trailer, you can use free video editing software like iMovie or Windows Movie Maker. Alternatively, you can outsource the task to a freelancer who can create a trailer for you. For other types of content, you can use free design tools like Canva to create graphics or record audio or video content using your smartphone or a free recording app.

Leveraging Social Media to Share Your Book Trailer and Other Multimedia Content

You can use social media to share your multimedia content with more people. Share your book trailer or other content on your own social media profiles or reach out to book bloggers, bookstagrammers, or other influencers in your genre and ask if they'll share your content with their followers. You can also try paid social media advertising to reach a larger audience.

Best Practices for Creating Effective Book Trailers and Other Multimedia Content

Here are some tips for creating compelling book trailers and other multimedia content:

- Keep your content brief and visually appealing
- Add sound effects or music to enhance the mood of your content
- Encourage viewers to take action, such as pre-ordering your book or visiting your website

- Ensure your content is consistent with the tone and style of your book

- Make your content easy to share and embed on social media and other websites.

104

Attend writing conferences and book events to network with other authors and industry professionals

Book fairs and literary events offer authors an incredible opportunity to establish connections with fellow writers and industry experts, as well as engage with readers and supporters. Some of the popular events include the London Book Fair, BookExpo America, Frankfurt Book Fair, and Edinburgh International Book Festival.

Advantages for Authors Attending Book Fairs and Literary Events

Book fairs and literary events offer authors numerous advantages. Firstly, they present an excellent opportunity to establish connections with fellow writers, agents, editors, and publishers in the industry. Additionally, authors can learn about the publishing sector's latest trends and advancements. Finally, these events can help authors showcase their work to a broader audience, interact with potential readers and fans, and promote their books.

Finding Writing Conferences and Book Events in Your Area

Finding writing conferences and book events in your area can be easy if you know where to look. One way is to conduct an online search using relevant keywords like "writing conferences" or "book events" and add your city or state to get results in your area. Additionally, you can check with local bookstores, libraries, and writing organizations to see if they have any upcoming events. Social media is another excellent resource for discovering events and connecting with other writers and industry professionals.

How to Find Book Signings, Readings, and Literary Events to Attend?

If you're looking for book signings, readings, and other literary events to attend, there are a few ways to find them. You can start by checking with your local bookstores, libraries, and literary organizations to see if they have any events coming up.

Another option is to follow your favorite authors and publishers on social media and sign up for their newsletters, as they often share news about upcoming events. You can also conduct an online search using relevant keywords like "writing conferences" or "book events" and add your city or state to get results in your area.

Finally, websites like Meetup.com and Eventbrite.com can also help you discover literary events in your area. By exploring these different options, you can find the perfect literary event to attend and connect with other book lovers in your community.

Ways to Network with Other Authors and Industry Professionals at Events

One way to network with other authors and industry professionals at these events is by attending workshops, panels, and Q&A sessions. You can also participate in networking events and meet-and-greet sessions. Having promotional materials and business cards can help you promote your work and connect with others. Following up with new connections after the event through email or social media can also help you build lasting relationships.

Preparing for a Writing Conference or Book Event

To have a successful experience at a writing conference or book event, preparation is key. Research the schedule of the event beforehand and decide which workshops or panels you want to attend. Remember to bring along plenty of business cards, pens, and a notebook to take notes. Dress professionally, but also make sure to wear comfortable shoes, as you may be on your feet for long periods. Lastly, practice your elevator pitch so that you can confidently introduce yourself and your work to others.

Tips for Making the Most out of a Writing Conference or Book Event

To make the most out of a writing conference or book event, it's essential to prioritize your time and focus on attending the panels and workshops that are most important to you. Be sure to engage with other attendees and industry professionals by asking questions and sharing your own experiences. Take thorough notes during panels and workshops, so you can remember what you've learned. After the event, follow up with any new connections you've made by sending a friendly message or connecting on social media. Attend networking events and meet-and-greet sessions to expand your network. Book signings are also beneficial.

You can also offer promotional materials like bookmarks with your website and social media information, and encourage readers to sign up for your newsletter. Offering signed copies of your book or hosting a giveaway can also help generate interest and create buzz around your work. By engaging with readers in a positive and authentic way, you can build a loyal fan base and grow your career as an author.

Tips for Authors Attending Their First Book Fair or Literary Event

For first-time attendees of book fairs and literary events, preparation and realistic expectations are crucial. Plan ahead, research the event and attendees and have a clear idea of who you want to meet and what you want to achieve. Being adaptable and open to unforeseen opportunities is vital.

Maximizing Time at Book Fairs and Literary Events as an Author

To fully maximize your experience at book fairs and literary events, prioritize your goals and manage your time wisely. Attend workshops and panel discussions that are relevant to your interests, connect with industry professionals, and engage with potential readers and fans. Be open to pitching your work and receptive to fresh ideas and diverse perspectives. Above all, remember to have fun and savour the experience!

How to Stand Out from Other Authors at Book Signings,

Readings, and Literary Events?

To make a memorable impression on readers and stand out from other authors at literary events, have a clear and captivating pitch for your book. Prepare to discuss what makes your book unique and why readers should be excited to read it. Visual aids or props can help bring your book's themes and setting to life, and dressing professionally and making eye contact with attendees can show your professionalism and confidence. You can also consider offering a special giveaway or hosting a unique event like a reading or book club discussion to make your presence at the event even more exciting. By being prepared and putting your best foot forward, you can make a lasting impression and gain new fans for your work.

Examples of Successful Book Signings, Readings, and Literary Events

There are several types of popular literary events that can help authors connect with readers and promote their work. Book clubs, author readings, and literary festivals are just a few examples. One notable event is the Texas Book Festival, which is among the largest literary events in the United States and offers author readings, panel discussions, and book signings. Another notable event is BookCon, which is a convention that brings together authors and readers for panel discussions, meet-and-greets, and book signings. Additionally, many local bookstores host author events and signings, providing a great opportunity for authors to engage with readers in their own community. By participating in these events, authors can connect with a wider audience and promote their work to new readers.

105

Don't be discouraged by rejection – keep submitting your work and looking for new opportunities to get it in front of readers.

Rejection is something that many writers experience and it can be disheartening. However, remember that being rejected doesn't mean you are a bad writer. Keep in mind that even the most successful writers have faced rejection at some point in their careers. It's just a normal part of the writing journey.

Common Reasons for Rejection in the Publishing Industry
There are various reasons why a publisher or literary agent may reject a manuscript. It could be because the manuscript doesn't match their preferences or standards. Alternatively, the writing may need more refining, or the story may not be interesting enough to capture their attention. It's also possible that the manuscript has potential, but it requires more effort to make it publishable.

How Many Submissions Before Giving Up on Your Work?

There's no universal rule for the number of submissions required before giving up on a manuscript. It's highly variable and depends on various factors. Sometimes, it may take multiple submissions before finding a suitable publisher or literary agent, while other times, it may be accepted on the first try. However, remember that every submission is a learning experience, and rejection shouldn't discourage you from improving your writing.

How Rejection Can Help You Improve as a Writer

Rejection can be a catalyst to enhance your writing skills and improve your manuscript. It can also offer constructive criticism that can be beneficial to your growth as a writer. When a rejection letter includes feedback, take it as a chance to learn and develop. Utilize the feedback to make your manuscript better and try submitting it again.

Ways to Stay Motivated After Receiving Rejection Letters

Maintaining motivation after getting rejected can be diffi-cult, but stay determined. One technique is to concentrate on any constructive feedback you obtain, whether it's from readers, beta readers, or writing partners. You can also take a break from your work and engage in new projects or participate in writing competitions or challenges. Additionally, make sure to commemorate your accomplishments, regardless of how minor they may seem. Every move ahead is a source of pride.

106

Consider hiring a publicist or marketing expert to help you with book promotion.

A publicist or marketing expert can aid authors with many aspects of promoting their book, including developing a marketing plan, arranging book tours and events, obtaining media coverage, managing social media and online presence, and designing promotional materials such as press releases and book trailers. They possess knowledge and skills in the publishing industry and can assist authors in navigating the intricate landscape of book marketing.

How to find a good publicist or marketing expert for your book

To find a good publicist or marketing expert, you need to invest some time in researching and exploring your options. You can start by asking other authors or professionals in the publishing industry for recommendations. Additionally, you can search online for marketing agencies or freelance publicists and read reviews and testimonials from their previous clients. Find someone who has experience in promoting books in your genre and can help you achieve your goals. Consider scheduling a consultation to discuss your expectations and determine if you have a good working relationship.

Qualities to look for in a publicist or marketing expert

When searching for a publicist or marketing expert, consider their expertise in your book's genre and audience, and their ability to tailor a marketing plan that highlights your book's unique features. Look for someone who is up-to-date with the latest trends in book marketing and has established connections in the publishing industry and media. Additionally, choose someone who is clear and open about their services and costs, and who communicates effectively with you throughout the process.

Costs of hiring a publicist or marketing expert

The cost of hiring a publicist or marketing expert depends on the services they offer and their level of expertise. Some charge a fixed amount for a particular package of services, while others work on a commission basis. It's essential to have a transparent conversation about your budget and goals and clarify which services are included in the fee.

Examples of successful book marketing campaigns run by experts

Publicists or marketing experts use various tactics for successful book marketing campaigns, such as arranging book tours, getting media coverage on various platforms, creating a buzz on social media, and collaborating with influencers and book bloggers. A publicist can help the author get featured on a popular TV show or podcast, or create a captivating book trailer that becomes a sensation on social media. However, the success of a book marketing campaign depends on several factors, including the book's quality, the author's interaction with their readers, and the effectiveness of the marketing strategy.

107

Don't rely solely on book sales – consider other revenue streams such as merchandising or speaking engagements

While selling books is important for authors to make money, there are also other ways to earn income. For instance, authors can sell merchandise, give speeches, or offer teaching or coaching services. These options can help authors make more money in addition to book sales.

Leveraging Merchandising to Promote an Author's Brand

Merchandising is a wonderful method for authors to boost their brand's visibility and engage with their audience in a unique way. For instance, authors can create merchandise showcasing their book covers, characters, or even their own catchphrases or logos. This can be an enjoyable way for authors to connect with their readers and create a community centered around their writing.

Examples of Merchandise Authors Can Sell

Authors have a wide range of merchandise to choose from, depending on their genre and audience. They can sell bookmarks, tote bags, t-shirts, mugs, or even jewellery. Authors can use their imagination and create distinctive items that relate to their brand and books.

Benefits of Speaking Engagements for Authors

Speaking engagements provide authors with a fantastic opportunity to meet their readers face-to-face and establish themselves as knowledgeable individuals in their field. It can also serve as an excellent source of revenue, as many events pay speakers for their time. Besides, speaking engagements can pave the way for other opportunities like book signings or interviews.

How to Secure Speaking Engagements as an Author

Authors can secure speaking engagements in several ways, such as by contacting event planners, pitching themselves as a speaker at conferences or book festivals, or collaborating with libraries or bookstores. Have a robust platform and a clear message to deliver to the audience. Therefore, authors should rehearse their presentations and be ready to discuss their work and knowledge with confidence.

108

Stay persistent and don't give up on your dream of becoming a published author.

Understand that obstacles and setbacks are common in this journey. Common obstacles include writer's block, lack of motivation, time management, and self-doubt. Writer's block is when you struggle to come up with new ideas or express your thoughts. Lack of motivation is when you can't find the energy or inspiration to write. Time management can be difficult when you have to balance writing with other responsibilities, and self-doubt can hold you back from pursuing your goals by making you question the quality of your work.

Staying motivated during the writing and publishing process

Staying motivated while writing and publishing can be challenging, but there are various ways to keep yourself inspired. Firstly, set achievable goals and deadlines to give yourself a clear path to follow. Secondly, surround yourself with positive people who support and motivate you. Thirdly, take breaks whenever you need them and avoid pushing yourself too much. Lastly, celebrate your accomplishments, no matter how small, such as finishing a chapter or receiving positive feedback from beta readers.

Dealing with rejection and criticism as an author
Receiving negative feedback or being turned down by publishers and readers is normal for writers. Instead of taking it to heart, use it to learn and become a better writer. Try not to take it personally and remember that everyone has different tastes. Writing is subjective, and what one person may not enjoy, another may absolutely love.

Success stories of authors who persevered despite setbacks
Many successful authors have faced rejection and obstacles but never gave up on their dreams. J.K. Rowling is a great inspiration for this, as she was turned down by many publishers before finally finding one for the Harry Potter series. Similarly, Stephen King faced rejection several times before getting published, yet he kept trying and didn't let rejection discourage him. These authors show that with determination and persistence, it's possible to achieve your goals.

Overcoming self-doubt and imposter syndrome as an author
Many writers experience self-doubt and imposter syndrome, but it's essential to realize that these feelings are just thoughts and not necessarily true. One way to overcome self-doubt is to focus on your strengths and accomplishments instead of your weaknesses. Surround yourself with people who believe in you and uplift you. Also, take good care of yourself, take breaks when you need to, and be gentle with yourself.

Finally, remember that every writer starts from somewhere, and nobody is perfect. Keep writing and improving, and you will see growth over time.

109

Create a professional author website to showcase your work and connect with readers.

An author website is crucial for writers because it acts as a central hub for their online presence. It helps readers to know more about the author and their works. It also helps authors to create their brand and promote their work. An author website can be a useful tool for readers to connect with authors and stay informed about their latest news and events.

Essential Elements for an Author Website

To create an effective author website, there are certain elements that you must include. Firstly, a brief and straight-forward biography that highlights your writing journey and personal background. Secondly, you should provide details about your books such as brief descriptions, reviews, and links to purchase them. You can also add a blog section where you can express your views on writing, publishing, and your personal life. Finally, make it easy for readers to connect with you by providing your contact information, such as an email address or a contact form.

Tips to Make Your Author Website Stand Out

To make your author's website unique and eye-catching, there are several steps you can take. Start by selecting a simple yet professional design that's easy to use and doesn't overwhelm your readers. Adding multimedia elements like pictures, videos, or audio recordings of you reading your work can also make your website more engaging. You could also consider offering exclusive content to your readers, such as bonus chapters, short stories, or behind-the-scenes glimpses of your writing process, to make your website more appealing.

Best Website Building Platforms for Authors

To create an author website, you can choose from different website-building platforms based on your budget and requirements. If you prefer a free option, you can opt for WordPress or Wix. But if you're willing to spend some money, Squarespace and Weebly are great alternatives that offer more advanced features and design templates. However, the ideal platform for you would depend on your technical skills and the particular features you're looking for.

Examples of Great Author Websites

There are many examples of successful author websites that you can look to for inspiration. One great example is Roxane Gay's website, which has a simple and stylish design and provides details about her books, public appearances, and writing courses. Another excellent author website is Neil Gaiman's, which features a lot of content, such as blog posts, audio recordings of his books, and videos. Finally, John Green's website is a good example of an author website that provides exclusive content, including autographed books and merchandise, as well as behind-the-scenes glimpses into his writing process.